Just Hospitality

Just Hospitality

God's Welcome in a World of Difference

Letty M. Russell

EDITED BY

J. Shannon Clarkson
and
Kate M. Ott

WESTMINSTER
JOHN KNOX PRESS
LOUISVILLE • KENTUCKY

First edition
Westminster John Knox Press
Louisville, Kentucky

09 10 11 12 13 14 15 16 17 18—10 9 8 7 6 5 4 3 2 1

Book design by Drew Stevens
Cover design by Lisa Buckley
Cover art by Yisehak F. Sellassie, Scripture Inspired Art "Kaleidoscope"
Yisehak Fine Arts, www.yisehakfinearts.com

Library of Congress Cataloging-in-Publication Data

Russell, Letty M.
  Just hospitality : God's welcome in a world of difference / Letty M. Russell ; edited by J. Shannon Clarkson and Kate M. Ott.—1st ed.
    p. cm.
  Includes indexes.
  ISBN 978-0-664-23315-0 (alk. paper)
  1. Hospitality—Religious aspects—Christianity. I. Shannon, Clarkson, J.
  II. Ott, Kate M. III. Title.
  BV4647.H67R87 2009
  241'.671—dc22

                                                                2008039364

To Eva and Isaac Ott Hill,
who brought Letty her last smile
with their Letty Bear drawing

Contents

Acknowledgments

We are most grateful to Westminster John Knox Press for honoring an enduring relationship—not only seeking to publish Letty M. Russell's fourteenth book with the press, but pairing us with our insightful and capable editor Stephanie Egnotovich. We benefited not only from her skill, but also her desire to create a text that honored Letty's work, aiding our struggle for comprehensiveness, cohesion, and clarity. Additional well-deserved thanks go to Hisako Kinukawa, Elizabeth Amoah, Aruna Gnanadason, Mary Hunt, Mercy Amba Oduyoye, and Phyllis Trible, who contributed clarity at points in the manuscript when our light dimmed. We are grateful to the many along the way who assisted us with finding resources of which Letty was aware, but we did not know; specifically, we must mention Pam Byers, Bear Ride, Susan Craig, and Ada María Isasi-Díaz.

Our thank-yous would not be complete without mentioning many others who, over the course of the project, walked with us in a variety of inspiring and caring ways. Our sincerest appreciation goes to Susan Meredith, John Watson, Holly and Eila Algood, Susan Ward, Annie Merkle, Jeanne Thomsen, and Brian Hill for their sustained friendship, enduring love, and continuing support. We, also, thank Margaret Farley, Kristen Leslie, Yolanda Smith, Emilie M. Townes, and David Maxwell for their generous spirits, encouraging words, and helpful hints as we moved into and through the process of bringing this book to life after the loss of our beloved colleague, mentor, friend, and partner. Midway through the revision process, we were able to share the theme and vision of the work with students of Starr King Seminary when Letty was posthumously awarded an honorary doctorate. Their enthusiasm for, and interest in, the work was inspiring and motivating.

Finally, we thank Letty. Her attention to details, including meticulous filing and MLA citation even in class lectures, made the task of compiling this manuscript manageable—and gave us many moments of laughter. It was an honor and a gift to have been part of bringing *Just Hospitality* to fruition.

Introduction

FROM MANY PARTS, A WHOLE

A theology of hospitality has always had three primary parts in Dr. Letty Russell's lectures, in her course design, and in her own practice. First, it is deeply rooted in a biblical understanding of the practice and meaning of hospitality. Second, inclusiveness as a mark of just hospitality must be balanced by analysis and awareness of differences in our lives. These differences are nuanced beyond the traditional markers of social location one might find in Dr. Russell's past work. Letty, which is what her students around the world called her, found a new way to talk about social identities, histories, and present relationships in a way that brought depth to how we work in community. This change is primarily due to her turn to postcolonial theory as she moved through the development of a theology of hospitality. Lastly, as in all of her work, a theological method of practice and theory is used. In other words, how we do hospitality (action) is as important as what we think about hospitality (reflection). Both serve to correct and expand traditional or stereotypical meanings for hospitality, challenging each of us to consider our lives as fertile ground for the doing of theology.

In chapter 1, Letty answers the question "why hospitality?" by demonstrating the action-reflection theological method. She uses the various events in her own life to explain how she arrived at her understanding of God's welcome, or just hospitality. Thus, her theological reflections are supported by concrete examples of her own practice of hospitality. For example, her experience in the World Council of Churches working globally with different Christian denominations informs her

xiii

discussion of dealing with differences and provides examples of how to practice just hospitality in difficult, yet real situations.

In chapter 2, Letty provides the reader with a detailed look at the method and theory behind her theological reflection. She uses a postcolonial theological perspective because it allows for a richer and more complex understanding of how difference functions in our individual and collective identities. This means we all bear the marks of a collective history that has formed us and need to sort out the power dynamics that stem from our differences.

Letty describes a richer sense of difference and a more complex understanding of how difference is created and used— biblically, historically, and today in our churches. The third chapter focuses on a biblical account of God's intention to create a world full of riotous difference—the story of the tower of Babel. Unfortunately, she observes, the church has historically viewed God's gift of difference as a problem and has responded accordingly. The resulting dualism and "othering" has created boundaries and reinforced the fear of the stranger, all of which impacts negatively the practice of a theology of hospitality. In response, Letty examines New Testament responses to difference and God's message to the early church regarding difference, in conjunction with how difference functions in our everyday lives.

In chapter 4, Letty reexamines existing ideas of hospitality, exploring their insufficiency and inappropriateness in a postcolonial world. She then reframes the idea of hospitality by identifying four central biblical components of hospitality— the unexpected divine presence, advocacy for the marginalized, mutual welcome, and creation of community. The notion of hospitality as a reaching across margins and partnering with strangers inevitably requires certain risks. Through a discussion of safety in scriptural texts and in how one reads Scripture, we are introduced to ways of looking for God's welcome in the midst of dangerous stories and situations.

In the final chapter, Letty defines and discusses precisely what she means by the term "just hospitality." Such hospitality includes solidarity and respect for differences that result from the history and social location of the other. The goal of just hospitality includes actions of genuine solidarity with those who are different from ourselves modeled on God's welcome. Based on human limits of our practice of hospitality, Letty suggests, with careful attention we can construct a network of hospitality that is truthful about our mistakes and power imbalances, and determined to resist the contradictions in our world and lives that drive us apart. As Letty says, "the sort of hospitality that makes this possible would be one that sees the struggle for justice as part and parcel of welcoming the stranger."

IN HONOR OF LETTY MANDEVILLE RUSSELL

It has been both an honor and a privilege to participate in the bringing of Letty's many years of writing on hospitality and even more years of practicing hospitality into a book she herself longed to complete. Letty would no doubt be embarrassed about the first chapter. She was never one to put herself before others, but these stories had been told, and we thought they were worth retelling—especially since hospitality could have been Letty's middle name. Although it doesn't always happen that one's theology and lifestyle are closely integrated, certainly that was the case with Letty.

Letty became (in)famous for her practice of Shalom Meals. At the end of each semester, students would come to Letty's home on the West River in Guilford, where they would join in a ritual of hospitality to close the months of learning and honor the beginnings of community they had formed. In most cases, a student group was in charge of designing and leading a worship which included singing songs, praying together, and a blessing of bread and wine. The meals were potluck style, and the evening included a time for toasts and celebrations where laughter and tears were plenty. Letty's practice of hospitality through Shalom Meals is one example of her open welcome to and sharing with students she saw as partners in the work of justice.

Letty was a rare person who actually lived what she preached and expected others to do so as well. She led by example, and on rare occasion she would tell you she was doing so. Letty passed away on July 12, 2007, in the peace of her home surrounded by family and friends. Many who read this book will do so because of a personal connection with Letty—as a teacher, mentor, or friend. Others of you may be hearing the name of Dr. Letty Russell for the first time. Reading Letty's theology is indeed like meeting her in person. She is a remarkable gift to the traditions of theological education, ecumenical movements, and most importantly the growth of global women's theologies. Letty was as comfortable talking about God in her living room as in a classroom, around a table in Cuba as on the floor in Indonesia, in the halls of Harvard and Yale as in the pews of East Harlem.

FOLLOWING THE CLUES

Several days after Letty died, Emilie Townes asked if there was enough material to finish Letty's book on hospitality. The immediate response was "No!" Letty's traditional way of writing was to accumulate hundreds of note cards upon which she had written references to articles, quotes from students, and her own thoughts and reflections about the topic. She would then shuffle and reshuffle the notes until she came up with a plan. The cards were around, but certainly not sorted. Letty spent many hours considering the order of material in her books, to say nothing of trying to make the chapter titles and subheads become a work of beauty in her eyes. She was fond of alliteration and concerned to make the sections and subsections meet her standard of formatting.

She was behind because she had devoted her last sabbatical to the "Save the Quad" campaign at Yale Divinity School. She and her colleague Margaret Farley, with help from a tiny band of alums, were in fact able to retain the Sterling Divinity Quadrangle for the school. Now Letty's portrait, and soon that of

Margaret Farley, graces the walls of the Common Room, along with previous deans of the seminary.

However, once again the moment of freedom of space and time for writing was thwarted when Letty was diagnosed with inoperable cancer. Yet rather than stopping all other activities to finally bring her hospitality book together, she chose, instead, to continue her immediate assignments: creating a prison ministry mentoring program for her parish, First Church UCC, Guilford, and writing and presenting the speech commitments and teaching assignments she had before her.

Perhaps she suspected that I, Shannon Clarkson her partner, and Kate Ott, Letty's former student and teaching assistant, would be able to find and follow her clues to her theology of hospitality. She always said that the sign of a good leader was to see who was following them and what they were doing. As you will see throughout the book, Letty uses the term "clues" quite often to refer to a signal, an insight, something that gives a reader of a biblical text or an examiner of personal experience an indication of how transformation might happen.

When Stephanie Egnotovich, Letty's editor, phoned asking the same question about Letty's book on hospitality, I modified my response and said I would check and see. Kate Ott and I turned on Letty's computer to see what was there. Not surprisingly, we found many files and folders related to hospitality. We found speeches, articles, class lectures, and notes. I had forgotten about the technological revolution that had transformed writing! Yet we still did not have an outline or those ever-important chapter titles and headings.

However, when we printed everything out and looked it over, an order emerged. Of course it helped that Kate had taken Letty's first course on hospitality and been a teaching assistant in subsequent ones! We then began to assemble the materials in the order in which Letty usually presented them. In the last year, Letty had often remarked that her book would be called "Just Hospitality." In the end, we fused Letty's primary title, "Just Hospitality," with subheadings we found time and again in her lectures and speeches on the subject: "God's

Welcome" and "A World of Riotous Difference." A few of the articles had been published, so are reprinted with permission. In the end, we have sometimes combined examples and elaborated explanations to provide a fuller treatment of the subject, but when possible have not changed her sentences.

We believe the world is different because Letty is gone from it. By the guidance of her spirit and the work of her theology, our hope is that the world will continue to be different through our work. *Just Hospitality* is not only a book to be read, but also a ministry to be practiced.

J. Shannon Clarkson and Kate M. Ott

1
Why Hospitality?

In this chapter I think through my own understanding of hospitality and its ability to address social structures of injustice and division in the world and in religious communities. I seek to connect action and reflection by asking about *all the ingredients* in our theology: experience, social reality, tradition, and action. In order to do this, I want to share with you some of my own experiences and insights. I will include how I came to the topic, an important clue from the biblical tradition, descriptions of hospitality, and last, possible clues about the integration of difference and community in ministries of hospitality. Then I will turn to the problems of using the practice of hospitality as a way to work for justice in a divided world.

Why hospitality? Of course, one answer to this question is as simple as what Christine Pohl, professor of church in society, says in *Making Room: Recovering Hospitality as a Christian Tradition*:

> Hospitality is not optional for Christians, nor is it limited to those who are specially gifted for it. It is, instead, a necessary practice in the community of faith.[1]

I understand hospitality as the practice of God's welcome, embodied in our actions as we reach across difference to participate with God in bringing justice and healing to our world in crisis. For me, my interest in hospitality began with and comes out of many years of work in the *ecumenical movement* and in ecumenical church structures. From 1977 to 1989, for instance, I was a member of the Faith and Order Commission, known as the theological think tank, of the World Council of Churches and of the National Council of the Churches of Christ, and worked on issues that divide the churches, such as doctrine and church order, or polity. I also spent a number of years working on the study *Baptism, Eucharist and Ministry.*[2] But despite the fact that those of us who were women, or who were from countries in the Global South—Asia, Africa, and Latin America— were present and asked to speak and write, our points of view were always considered a problem *because we increased the diversity of opinion concerning faith and order.* This was particularly the case for women in ministry, those who had been ordained. Again and again their comments appeared only in the footnotes, if at all! They were truly in the margin.

As bell hooks has made so clear in such writings as *Feminist Theory: From Margin to Center*, margins are socially constructed sites that dominant groups consider to be the location of those who are of "no account."[3] These margins are not always easy to locate, because they (and the social, political, economic, and ecclesial power they represent) keep shifting as people gain and lose power in movement from center to margin. But margins can be places of connection for those who are willing to move from the center out. They are sites of struggle for those who choose the margin but move to the center in order to gain the ability to talk back.[4] And when the distinctions of margin and center begin to blur, as all share in God's hospitality, we are being given the sign that God's New Creation is breaking in.

My discipline of liberation and feminist theologies involves knowing where the margin and center are located in order to respond appropriately. My own intellectual, social, personal, and political biography is full of those margins and centers, and I am constantly on the move to find the margin and to claim it as the site of my theology of resistance. Theologians like myself make choices about moving from margin toward center, or from center toward margin, according to where we find ourselves in relation to the center of power and resources, and of cultural and linguistic dominance in any particular social structure. Our connection to the margin is always related to where we are standing in regard to social privilege, and from that particular position we have at least three choices. The first is to live where we are and refuse to challenge the social construction of our identity in terms of class, gender, sexuality, or race. The second is to choose the margin and work for the empowerment of people who have been themselves marginalized by the dominant cultural, political, economic, religious, or educational systems. The third choice is to identify with those in power in the center and to emulate the dominant group.[5]

In this chapter, I want to look at the various social locations of my own life and work, asking in what way they pushed me to keep moving to the margin as part of my commitment to share in Christ's welcome of all persons into God's household or reign. First, I will describe how *growing up in the center* helped to shape my theology and provide me with the roots of my Christian faith and commitment. Then I will revisit my experience of *living in the margins* that shaped the themes of my theological reflection, teaching, and writing. Finally I will look at the ways in which my work has become more and more identified with *struggling in the center* of the elitism at Yale University.

ON BEING A MISFIT: EMBRACING HOSPITALITY

I don't know if I am an "outsider within" or an "insider without," but I do know that I have always been a misfit! I have been a misfit for my entire life and ministry as an educator, pastor, ecumenist, and theologian. This is a very common experience for groups of persons who "miss the mark" because they are not white, Euro-American, affluent, heterosexual, able-bodied, or male.

I have served within the structures of the Presbyterian Church and various ecumenical and academic institutions, yet even as I did, I have always known that there is something that makes me a "square peg in a round hole." My woman's body and woman's way of work somehow do not measure up to the father stereotype of a Protestant pastor. Even today, with ever increasing numbers of talented and gracious women in church leadership, the question of where they fit into the male-dominated hierarchy of the church is ever with us.

In the midst of social structures designed to push out, or down, anyone who does not fit into the right model because of race, class, nationality, gender, or sexual orientation, I have discovered many networks of wonderful people devoted to the work of justice and partnership in the mission of the church in the world. Moreover, over the years many changes have taken place in the church in the United States and abroad, one of them being the increasing contribution of outsiders to what has until now been a white, Eurocentric, male church. This I celebrate as I reflect on my own journey as a woman who is *in but still out* of the church, and how that has led me to search for clues to the meaning of our call to ministry in a church inside out. My experience as an outsider within has also led me to embrace a ministry of hospitality.

In But Still Out

In 1973 Elizabeth Howell Verdesi published a book on the history of women's work in the Presbyterian Church entitled *In But Still Out: Women in the Church.*[6] She identified and documented two events in which women in the denomination lost their access to power and decision making. First, in the 1920s, the Women's Board of Missions found itself restructured into the boards and agencies of the church and no longer in control of either its finances or the work of women in mission. Then, in the 1940s and 1950s the women had a potential power base in Christian education but allowed it to be co-opted by the larger structures of the church.

We know that there are many reasons for such events/ reorganizations—they continue to happen today—but we also know that the experience of women in the church has on occasion been an experience of diminishment and restructuring, if not downright hostility. The General Assemblies are regularly the scene of strategies to contain efforts to empower young women and reach out in new ways to the coming generations. This sort of political action by those who are in competition to control church structures affects the role of lay women as well as those who are ordained deacons, elders, and ministers of the Word and Sacrament.

Making sense of what ministry means for women and men within structures of oppression or marginality that are the result of racism, sexism, and classism has been one of my lifelong concerns. In fact, it has been my concern for so long that the list of isms keeps growing—with imperialism, ableism, heterosexism, globalization, environmental destruction, now added to the list! Nor have I been able to ignore the fact that as an educated, white, Euro-American woman I benefit from many of the privileges that come from such social sins. Yet I am always status inconsistent: a woman who has authority in the church as a pastor and theologian, but also a bisexual[7] feminist who advocates for the full humanity of *all* women, together with *all* men in harmony with the creation.

Making Sense of Myself

I must confess that my critical perspective on theology developed at a very early age. I grew up attending a Presbyterian church in Westfield, New Jersey, a largely white, middle-class town in northern New Jersey. My parents expected me to attend church school and/or church each Sunday, but while still in kindergarten I ran away from church school and made my way home across a number of forbidden streets. On my arrival home I greeted my startled mother with the comment,

"There just is nothing there to interest a girl like me!" Interesting or not, that church remained my theological home all the way through high school, although I drew the line at attending the youth group; the Jack Benny radio program was more fun.

My church and my family were, I know, important to the development of my faith in Jesus Christ and my trust in God's love. But it was only much later, when I began to study religion in college, that I began to notice the long tradition of church involvement on both sides of my family that was my heritage. Although my father seldom attended church, his grandmother in Boston, Mary Luny Russell Charpiot, with whom he grew up, founded the Massachusetts Home for Intemperate Women in Boston in 1881. The home housed 100 women and was the first of its kind in the United States. My mother often stayed home on Sunday with my father, but her parents were pillars of the local church, and she herself became an active lay leader after my father died.

I trace my feminist tendencies to the fact that I always felt like a *misfit*. As a child, I wanted to play active games and was what they used to call a tomboy. I refused to learn to read until I was in the fourth grade, because the books about "Dick and Jane" were so boring. One day I discovered a great book on the Vikings and read it cover to cover. The next day I told the teacher I could read and wanted to be put up in the highest reading group! By seventh grade I was already 5' 8", the tallest girl in the class; a tomboy who did not fit!

What was it that gave me a *sense of entitlement*, even though I often did not fit the stereotypes of white, middle-class America? One very important factor was undoubtedly that I grew up as the "boy" in a family with three girls and never felt any pressure from my parents to forsake my interest in woodworking, sports, or anything else that wasn't the typical domain of girls. I discovered the pain of this type of behavior only when I got to adolescence. In junior high school, I towered over all the other seventh graders. When the students asked me to play "Pistol Packing Mama" in the school musical I knew what it meant to be different! Yet, in spite of clearly being different, I continued to think of myself as having a great deal of entitlement.

As the speaker at my high-school graduation I took the opportunity to talk about the idea of noblesse oblige. What led me to this strong sense of our responsibility to others? Most certainly it was at the heart of what I learned in my family and in my religious education. My role model was my grand-mother, Letty Mandeville Towl, who labored all her life in tire-less service to her family, community, and church. Her love for others blanketed me as well, so that, although I had a strong sense of autonomy and independence, I knew that the love and care I received and experienced from her was what life should be about. I am particularly grateful for her, because my father was a very rigid person whose anger at any infringement of his authority could easily have shaped me in a different way.

I grew up with an orthodox Presbyterian theology, which I never took seriously enough to reject. I knew very early that there were different opinions about things because my father was a Unitarian and spent Sundays at the tennis club and not in church. Clearly, the part of my faith that was most nurtured within my family was service to others and responsibility for one's own actions before God.

When I followed my Mother's footsteps and went to Welles-ley College, I thought I would fit right in. And it seemed only right, therefore, that I would arrive at Wellesley to find its motto, *non ministrari, sed ministrare* (not to be ministered unto, but to minister), emblazoned on its crest and across the chapel chancel. My sense of entitlement had always incorporated the assumption I would go to college. At Wellesley I also had a strong and continuing role model in President Mildred McAfee Horton. Having served as commander-in-chief of the WAVES in World War II, she was already a role model for the heroic behavior that I'd admired as a child during the war, when I wanted so much to be old enough to serve in the WAVES! Again, she was a strong, caring, faithful woman who lived out Wellesley's motto day by day. I had chosen a school where as a white woman I would not be a misfit, but I found that my father's lower economic status and my interest in religion made me somewhat "different." This *difference*, I've always felt, was the foundation of my life of Christian service.

But the most important role models I had were my peers who lived with me in the co-op dorm as scholarship students. I found myself living with the daughters of ministers, missionaries, and teachers who could not afford Wellesley's tuition. This businessman's daughter who thought she had escaped compulsory church attendance on high school graduation found herself singing in the chapel choir, daily and Sunday! The one who had thought church was boring was soon involved in a biblical history major, with extracurricular activities centered in the ecumenical religious life on campus, and in the Student Christian Movement (SCM) of New England. One day on the train to New York I told my father that I was going to work in the church as a Christian educator. His reply? "You'll be sorry because *you will always be a misfit!*"

If my Father thought religion was marginal to what counts in society, there were many people at Wellesley who did not share this opinion, including women who were teaching theology, church history, ethics, Bible, and philosophy with no thought of gender inequality. My church history professor was Louise Pettibone Smith, a social activist and exacting scholar who in 1913 became the first woman to publish in the *Journal of Biblical Literature* of the Society of Biblical Literature. She was also the only woman to appear in its pages in its first forty years![8] One of my Bible professors was Lucetta Mowry, later to be the first woman on both the RSV and the NRSV New Testament translation committees. Neo-orthodoxy reigned in the theology department, but this sounded like the scholarly footnotes for my Presbyterian heritage. The most important theological shift in college was ecumenical theology. As an officer in the Student Christian Movement of New England, I planned and attended conferences and became deeply involved in trying to connect the work of the church to a worldwide movement for peace and for social justice.

LIVING ON THE MARGINS

When I graduated from Wellesley, I reached for the center but soon found myself living in the margins. Through my ecumenical connections and work at SCM, I'd met and then married one of SCM's coleaders, a student at Harvard. Following the middle-class prescription for a white woman in 1951, I graduated, got married, and moved to Higganum, Connecticut, to teach school and serve as a pastor's wife while my husband began his studies at Yale Divinity School. But this prescription didn't seem to fit me very well. I knew something was wrong when my Methodist husband was not sure he wanted to be married to me if I believed in "predestination." By the end of our first year of marriage, he had left Yale and abandoned me, leaving me to care for his church as student pastor and continue teaching my third-grade class.

In the pain of these events, I recognized that if I could not fulfill my Christian vocation by being a pastor's wife, I could do it by entering ministry on my own. And so I ended up in the most challenging place I could find: an ecumenical parish in East Harlem where some of my friends in the Student Christian Movement were already at work. At least there I could learn more about who I was by living in a different culture and by finding ways to carry out Jesus' words, "not to be served, but to serve" (Matt. 20:28). I found a home at this church in the margins of an interracial, low-income ghetto. By raising my salary from my home church in New Jersey I was able to fund my position as a Christian education director and become a home missionary of the United Presbyterian Church.

Coming to East Harlem was like coming home—not just because my college roommate came to work with me in the East Harlem Protestant Parish (EHPP) as her field placement from Union Theological Seminary, or just because I was coming out of a soul-searching crisis and life change. It was home because I discovered among this marginalized community that in God's sight no one is a misfit and that it is our call to join God in practicing hospitality for all persons. The community of the Church of the Ascension where I was working and of the Group Ministry of EHPP welcomed my gifts as a teacher and minister and became my extended family.

Nevertheless, I soon found that I needed a seminary education. It was clear that my calling was to work in the church, and for that I needed an advanced degree. I also needed more extensive theological tools in order to be able to connect our daily struggles for life with the teachings of Scripture and tradition. My critical perspective was also beginning to make me increasingly aware of power issues, and it did not take me long to notice that, even in a group ministry where everyone is "equal," one needed to be a pastor in order to carry out reforms that connected education and action with the worship life of the church. In a clerical church structure, ordination is the "union card" needed to conduct the worship and determine the direction of where the church is headed.

I chose to attend Harvard Divinity School because I needed space away from my East Harlem involvement and I had been supervising Union Theological Seminary students for three years. I was also excited about Harvard Divinity's reorganization under President Nathan Pusey. The renewed program was headed up by Dean Douglas Horton, the husband of my mentor, Mildred McAfee Horton, and Paul Tillich and George Buttrick were on the faculty. Ignoring the fact that Harvard Divinity School did not admit women, I wrote and applied and said they should change their rules. They did change, and I entered as one of two women in the MDiv program, then called a Bachelor of Divinity degree. They moved Judith Hoehler and me into the maid's quarters in the home of the dean and his wife, and that was where we began our studies!

At Harvard there was no mistaking the fact that I was marginal. Most of the time I was the only woman in class, and the only student addressed by a first name. My professors and friends were all men. I didn't think any of this made a lot of difference, because I was there to gain the biblical tools I needed from professors such as Amos Wilder, Frank Cross, and Krister Stendahl, and the critical tools for understanding ways of interpreting gospel and culture from Paul Lehmann and Paul Tillich. The most important question I faced was how to interpret ethics and the teachings of the church in different social settings. Tillich's early work on the *Protestant Era* had inspired us in East Harlem to look for new ways of being a church engaged with social issues, and Lehmann's contextual ethics held the possibility of making ethical sense in an oppressed community such as East Harlem.

Just how marginal I was became apparent only in retrospect, when I learned that having two women graduating at the head of the class created a problem: some of my professors were reluctant to grant top honors to us because it would reflect badly on the qualifications of the men!

The Presbyterian Church U.S.A. was not much better. It had only begun ordaining women in 1956 and had no jobs for women pastors. Many other women and men had also caught the spirit of reform, however, and, after I graduated, I was able to become the first woman approved for ordination in my presbytery. In 1958 I returned to the East Harlem Protestant Parish, where I was ordained as a pastor of the Presbyterian Church of the Ascension. My call to serve this church was truly a lucky one for me, for in spite of my connections to power through whiteness, education, and now ordination, I continued to be accepted as "just Letty."

My work as a pastor in the 1960s involved me heavily in the civil rights movement and led me to develop a strongly biblical theology of liberation. I was the author of the Daily Bible Reading lectionary for inner-city parishes for eight years.[9] At the same time I became a member of the World Council of Churches' working group on the Missionary Structure of the Congregation. This ecumenical work, particularly in the area of church renewal on the mission structure study and in the Faith and Order Commission of the WCC and the Community of Women and Men Study of the WCC, has continued to shape my theology.

After seventeen years in East Harlem I finished my ThD at Union Theological Seminary, married Hans Hoekendijk, and went to teach at the Christian Brothers' Manhattan College in the Bronx. When I was interviewed at what was then a men's college, the Brother who was president was disappointed because I was not African American and represented only two outsider slots: woman and Protestant. He said to me, "Who are you anyway?" I answered him, "I am a father, Brother!" They must have been hard up because I got the job.

Becoming a Feminist

For me, there has never been any separation between my religious faith and the feminist movement. Those of us who struggle for empowerment in church institutions are simply part of the larger and very diverse movement for the inclusion and empowerment of women in all fields and in all parts of the world. The feminist movement has helped to make sense of what is a common experience for many outsiders and oppressed groups, because it names the contradictions in our lives so that we can see them and work with others in the struggle to change them.

Feminism came into my life in the late 1960s while I was in East Harlem and engaged in the struggles of the civil rights movement. When I read Betty Friedan and Mary Daly, I knew right away that they were describing another structure of oppression. This one included me in both the oppressed group and the oppressor group. I began writing women's liberation material for the church and the national board of the YWCA in the early seventies, and joined other women in the ecumenical movement to create an international women's network through the World Council of Churches. I made sense of my experience in justice work and my experience as a woman by writing *Human Liberation in a Feminist Perspective: A Theology*,[10] which was also the title of a course I was teaching at Yale Divinity School in 1974. I tried to show that liberation theology, black theology, and feminist theology share the same liberating roots in the Christian tradition and that, as they say, "no one is free until all are free."

That book grew out of a network of resistance and struggle in the World Council of Churches (WCC), where I was involved in a study on "Christians in Changing Institutions." The WCC refused to include a feminist group in the study, so I created one in New York City and met with women at Union Theological Seminary and at the Interchurch Center to examine how Christian women *were* changing institutions! I wrote a report. Always needing reports, the WCC published it under the title "Human Liberation in a Feminine Perspective." That feminist group was the beginning of a network that continued to work to change the WCC. The group called itself WOW: Women of the World and was successful in its campaign to mandate that all WCC committees at the 1975 Nairobi Assembly consist of 25 percent women (rather than the existing 2 percent). We briefly became POW, Participation of Women, because although the churches appointed more women, they refused to fund their participation in meetings. We raised enough funds to send nearly all the women to the WCC Assembly in Nairobi. Afterward, we changed our name to RSAC (Ad Hoc Group on Racism, Sexism, and Classism) and we have kept on going ever since! Thirty years later we have added *ageism* to our title!

The Gift of Not Fitting

Through the feminist movement I discovered that being a misfit can be a gift and the opportunity for *a revolution of small changes*.[11] Being a misfit allows us to understand the meaning of hospitality and honor difference from the side of the stranger. When I speak of God's welcoming of the stranger and our partnership in this welcoming action toward all religions, races, and genders, I can do so, at least in part, as one who claims what postcolonial feminists call *hybridity*. By that I mean that I am *both outside and within* institutional power structures. As an advocate of peace with justice, I can work with others for the empowerment of all peoples, "regardless."

Practicing God's hospitality means that I am constantly looking for ways to empower other outsiders in the institutions where I work and live. I always have to ask myself as I gather with a group, "Who is missing? Who are the ones whose voice is not heard?" As a Christian I learned to do this from the gospel message of Jesus Christ, and I have found that these questions also help to make sense of the rhetoric of the feminist movement. In 1988, for instance, I joined Mercy Oduyoye, Ada María Isasi-Díaz, and Kwok Pui-lan in inviting women to tell the stories of their mothers. We were, in the process, encouraging women to find their own identity and self-worth and to honor their own way of thinking theologically, and our efforts resulted in a book entitled *Inheriting Our Mothers' Gardens*,[12] providing an opportunity for women writers of color to break into publishing and become outsiders within.

I value being an outsider within because it keeps me on edge, looking for the *power quotient* in any situation, and struggling for change. In fact, I worried about going to teach at Yale in 1972 because my own racial and class background fit in too well. But I need not have worried! A lesbian teaching feminist, queer, and liberation theologies is not quite that old norm. Here I was "a triangular peg in a round hole." The faculty always wondered how I managed to get in, and I always was determined to make the most of it!

I learned in East Harlem, and and have had the lesson reinforced many times since, that in God's sight no one is a misfit and I thank God for the second women's movement and the opportunity to be part of the goal of making sense of women's lives. Even in my retirement I remain an outsider within; Yale managed to make me *a misfit forever* by giving me a certificate of retirement that described me in male terms. Unable to write Latin correctly or to think that a woman might have been around long enough to retire, they wrote on my certificate, professor of theology *emeritus*! When last heard from, they had not figured out how to change my title to *emerita*. At least the church has simply allowed me to be honorably retired.

THE CHURCH INSIDE OUT

In 1966 my late husband, Hans Hoekendijk, published a book entitled *The Church Inside Out*,[13] in which he argued that God is at work in the world to mend the creation and that the church does not have a separate mission but is, instead, invited to be part of God's mission and to witness to God's love in the world. This perspective can help us to make sense of what ministry is all about: The ministry is not ours. Nor does it belong to the church. Rather the ministry of service to humankind is the ministry of God in Christ reconciling the world. The church is invited to participate in that ministry. Yet in many churches the minister's job is perceived to be taking care of the flock, rather than equipping the saints for their service in the world. I have long wondered why the church is so preoccupied with what is *inside* itself, and forgets God's concern for justice or putting things right in the world; our table of hospitality is only for the insiders.

Paul's call in 1 Corinthians 7:29–31 is for Christians to be "In, but not of, the world." He is reminding the Corinthians that while they are to continue to *participate* in the ongoing life of their communities, they are to live as if the New Creation were already at hand.[14] This call is frequently ignored in our churches today, and many Christians live *of, but not in, the world*. They are "of the world" because their lives, structures, class divisions, sexual orientation, and prejudices all reflect the culture of which they are a part. They are "not in the world," however, because they refuse the task of witnessing to God's intention for the New Creation by not practicing works of justice and peace and extending hospitality.

To be a church inside out we cannot ignore issues of social sin and focus on personal morality while reducing spirituality to a search for salvation. We must instead open our lives to God by practicing a wholistic spirituality of connection to God, to our own bodies and ourselves, and to our neighbors in need, be they next door or on the other side of the world. Participating in the already, not yet of God's New Creation leads to bold initiatives to bring peace and justice to the world.

The Church in the Round

In my ministry as a theologian and teacher I have tried to find ways to make the church more open to the needs of the whole world. In my book *Church in the Round: A Feminist Interpretation of the Church*, I described the church as "a community of Christ, bought with a price, where everyone is welcome."[15] It is a community of Christ because Christ's presence, through the power of the Spirit, constitutes people as a community gathered in Christ's name (Matt. 18:20; 1 Cor. 12:4–6). This community is bought with a price because the struggle of Jesus to overcome the structures of sin and death constitutes both the source of new life in the community and its own mandate to continue the same struggle for life on behalf of others (1 Cor. 6:20; Phil. 2:1–11). Everyone is welcome here because they gather around the Table of God's hospitality. The welcome Table is a sign of the coming feast of God's mended creation, and its guest list is inspired by the announcements of the jubilee year in ancient Israel—"But when you give a banquet, invite the poor, the crippled, the lame, and the blind" (Luke 14:13).

Ministry in such a church would be a roundtable ministry that seeks to be open to those at the margins of church and society. It would work to include those who have historically been excluded from the leadership of the church because of their race, gender, or sexual orientation. During my years in ministry I have frequently participated in ecumenical discussions on ordination. In most of these discussions, such as those in the World Council of Churches' Faith and Order Commission (which I discuss in *Church in the Round*),[16] the focus was on the limits of ordination, the boundaries that churches have set concerning who is qualified or disqualified for a ministry of the Word and Sacrament. Many of these meetings were about "the problem" of women's ordination. As far as I was concerned, there was no problem with women in ministry, as I had been serving as a minister for over twenty years.

The 1979 Consultation of Faith and Order in Strasbourg, France, was the first meeting in which the gathered theologians and church officials were willing to recognize that it was ordination that was the problem and not women! The problem was the church's reluctance to change *its* traditions to include women. In ecumenical settings, the fact that some denominations ordain women does not solve the problem. Until all are included equally, the ecclesiastical body of Christianity remains broken. The interpretations of ministry to ordain women or not were doctrinally sound according to church tradition, but the idea of ministry as Christ's continuing ministry of service had been lost in the tangle of doctrinal and structural boundaries. The admission that ordination was the problem, and not women, was such a shift that I wrote about it afterward as *the Strasbourg shift*.[17] It is now time to stop asking, "Why should women or queer people be ordained?" and instead ask, "Why should anyone be ordained as long as the structures divide lay and clergy persons and set up a hierarchy in the church?"

One Call, Many Ministries

For a church in the round that seeks to be partners with those at the margins of church and society, ministry is an expression of Jesus Christ's continuing service in the world. Rather than protecting Christ's ministry by restricting it to church hierarchies and separating it from the needs of the world, the church in the round welcomes the possibility that all may freely serve. Christians share in the ministry of Jesus, who came not to be served, but to serve (Matt. 20:25–28). The ways we participate in that ministry are varied and change from time to time, but we are all baptized into it and continue to serve God and neighbor our entire lifetime.

Baptism is the basic ordination of all Christians, and the ordination of a person as deacon, elder, or minister of Word and Sacrament is the way in which a particular community recognizes that person's gift to equip the rest of us for ministry. In the Presbyterian Church, a person's call to pastoral ministry is discerned by asking whether they have experienced an internal call by the Holy Spirit; whether they have the gifts, education, and experience for a particular form of ministry; and whether the church community has need of these gifts and ways to sustain that ministry. This kind of discernment process happens over and over in our lives, and our ministries change in response to the needs of the church and world. With the many shifts in the ways we are called to serve, the Strasbourg shift alerts us to a need to reexamine whether particular ministries require ordination for life.

What is for life, however, is the sacrament of baptism, which is a sign of God's call in our life. Whether we deny that call or run away from it, God's call is always with us through many ministries. Whether this service is in the church or not, whether it is paid or not, whether it is clerical or not, a particular ministry is one of many ways of living out the one calling of God in Jesus Christ. In my own life I have been in many different ministries, and I intend to continue seeking out new needs and ways of service in response to my call. This is why I like to talk about my *rewirement* rather than *retirement*. There is no way that I or any other Christian can retire from our many ministries of service.

MINISTRY OF HOSPITALITY

My experience as an outsider within has clearly led me to question the rigid clergy line that divides our church communities and increases hierarchy and competition for power in our denomination. At the same time, it has led me to focus on a theology of hospitality that emphasizes the calling of the church as a witness to God's intention to mend the creation by bringing about a world of justice, peace, and integrity of the natural world. There are a lot of "missing persons" in our world today whose situation of poverty, injustice, and suffering makes God weep. These missing persons are not strangers to God, for God already has reached out to care for them. Yet they are strangers in the world who need to know God cares through the witness of a church that practices a ministry of hospitality and justice on their behalf.

Hospitality

What do we mean by hospitality? In the church we often think of hospitality as what the women offer after the worship service on Sunday. We do not think of this as a form of ministry but rather assume it means "tea and crumpets." In other contexts, the idea of hospitality is reduced to sexual services offered by "ladies of the night."

Although hospitality is a form of Christian spirituality and is basic to the biblical message, the practice of the biblical injunction for hospitality has fallen into disuse in our churches and society.[18] Hospitality is the practice of God's welcome by reaching across difference to participate in God's actions bringing justice and healing to our world in crisis. Such action is not easy. Yet the biblical witness is clear: The unexpected presence of God and Christ in and through actions of hospitality is seen in Abraham and Sarah's hospitality to divine messengers at the oaks of Mamre and the discovery of the risen Christ in the breaking of bread in Emmaus (Gen. 18:1–15; Luke 24:13–35). Hebrews 13:2 reminds us, "Do not neglect to show hospitality to strangers, for by doing that some have entertained angels without knowing it." The many injunctions to practice hospitality to the widow, the orphan, and the stranger, in thanksgiving for Israel's deliverance from bondage and for God's gifts, remind us that we have been strangers who are welcomed by God and are to welcome others in return (Exod. 23:9). This practice of hospitality is the ministry of all the members of a congregation and not just church women's groups, welcoming committees, or clergy.

In Matthew 25:31–46 Jesus promises to be with those who offer hospitality to the least of our brothers and sisters. From this it would seem that hospitality can be understood as *solidarity with strangers*, a mutual relationship of care and trust in which we share in the struggle for empowerment, dignity, and fullness of life. The word for hospitality in the Greek New Testament is *philoxenia*, love of the stranger. Its opposite is *xenophobia*, hatred of the stranger.[19] The ministry of the church is to be partners with strangers, to welcome those whom Christ welcomed, and thus learn to be a community in which people are made one in Jesus Christ in spite of their different classes, religious backgrounds, genders, races, and ethnic groups. Our koinonia or partnership in Christ is a gift of our baptism and not a result of being of one class, race, or sexual orientation. It is a gift that transcends real differences through participation in the mission and ministry of the church on behalf of healing the brokenness of the world, beginning with ourselves.

Difference

My favorite definition of difference is an "archaic" definition from *Webster's Online Dictionary: a characteristic that distinguishes one from another or from the average.* Difference is *not just diversity* or variety in general. It refers to concrete elements in our lives that separate, distinguish, or contrast one group or person from another.

Hospitality is a two-way street of mutual ministry where we often exchange roles and learn the most from those whom we considered different or "other."[20] This has been true for me in my solidarity with women in the Circle of Concerned African Women Theologians,[21] a partnership that began in early 2002 between the Circle women and some of us at Yale Divinity School and the Yale Center for Interdisciplinary Research on AIDS. The general topic of the work of these theologians was "Sex, Stigma and HIV/AIDS: African Women Theologians Challenging Religion, Culture and Social Practices," and our work together focused on their research, projects, and publications related to these issues. We have worked together in particular to find U.S. publishing venues for the Circle writings, and establish postdoctoral fellowships to study at Yale. During the fellowship, the women design qualitative research projects to administer when they return home that will change the attitude of churches about issues of prevention and care for persons living with HIV/AIDS.[22] Sharing in the experiences the women bring to their projects, as they claim their own power to name both the problems and solutions to the difficulties they face, has challenged me to be both a learner and a teacher in the struggle to face what has become a global AIDS pandemic.

In our fractured world and church, the problems of difference are never absent. Economic globalization forces people to migrate from one place to another to escape war, poverty, sickness, genocide, and more. We are often strangers to one another, but the problem that we face is not that we are different, but that we often fear that difference and reject those outside our church, our community, our nation. This fear of difference has even been used by those in power as an excuse to oppress those who are of a different nationality, race, gender, sexual orientation, or ability. And churches unfortunately reinforce this fear and rejection by becoming "safe havens" from difference, welcoming only certain groups and misusing theological teachings to exclude those who don't fit.

I continue to understand my ministry in the Presbyterian Church (U.S.A.) from the perspective of an *outsider within*. I am glad to be in this position, however, because it forces me continually to challenge the church to be a *church inside out* and to challenge myself to practice a ministry of just hospitality. I was ordained in East Harlem in 1958 because I knew that I needed to be ordained in order to be able to integrate the worship life of the church with its educational ministry and justice advocacy. When I left East Harlem seventeen years later to begin my teaching ministry, I continued to be ordained because I was simply *rewiring* and changing the location of my ministry.

Although I believe that the structures of lifelong ordination should be reformed, I also believe that, as long as this process is the avenue to church leadership, all baptized Christians should be welcome to offer their gifts within and beyond the structures of the church. In particular I have continued to be ordained because it has allowed me to be a model for women who are denied access to a ministry of Word and Sacrament in other denominations. In addition, my ordination serves as a continual reminder to my own denomination that sexual orientation is no barrier to the exercise of the gifts of the Holy Spirit. In spite of all the mixed messages of hierarchy and privilege that go with ordination, the practice of ministry has been a blessing in my life, and I give thanks for the continuing experience of God's call to hospitality to all. As we pray for the renewal of the church as an instrument of justice and peace in the world, we must stand in solidarity with strangers by working against the oppressive structures that make them outsiders within their own societies. In the process we may discover God's hospitality in our own communities.

Questions for Thought

1. Where do you most often find yourself, based on your gender, race, class, sexual orientation, age, and ability: in the center, at the margin, or moving in between?
2. How does your location shape your faith and commitments?
3. What personal experiences have helped you to define hospitality?
4. Think about the phrase "That all may freely serve." Does your faith community offer a variety of ways for different people to serve? What are these opportunities? What might be other ways ministries of hospitality could be expanded to be more inclusive?

2

The New Hospitality

In 2001, the American Academy of Religion honored Gustavo Gutiérrez on the thirtieth anniversary of the publication of his book *A Theology of Liberation*.[1] In his response to the panel Professor Gutiérrez pointed out that theologies are always changing, because they cannot be separated from the historical process. Our new situation, he said, is that we are "post" everything, that we love to be post, but we do not live in a post racist, sexist, classist, imperialist world.

This is the dilemma that we all face regarding the future! We seek to be postmodern but the legacy of modernity and the Enlightenment is all around us. We seek to be postcolonial but are surrounded by various forms of colonialism and imperialism. In the church, as we think about hospitality, we try to be both *postpatriarchal* and *postimperial* in our discussions of mission and our colonial past in establishing missions, yet we often get only as far as examining the "otherness" of those who are not Eurocentric white males.

In the past, like Gutiérrez, I have used a hermeneutic of the "other," writing as one who is implicated on both sides of otherness, yet feminist postcolonial analysis has led me to a hermeneutic of hospitality, which is a newer and still unfolding practice. A hermeneutic of the other would highlight, on the one hand, my position as an educated, white, North American university professor who has all the privileges that allow me to think of uneducated people from nations in the Southern Hemisphere, as well as their descendants and Native Americans in the United States, as "other." But I am also a lesbian woman who finds herself often marginalized as "other" by those who hold only to a heterosexual, male definition of normal. And, as one who began her professional career as a home missionary in the slums of East Harlem fifty years ago, I have long been involved in the struggle to find ways to live out a sharing of power across racial and economic lines. I have decided to move my thinking from "hermeneutic of the other" to a *hermeneutic of hospitality* because as a feminist theologian I no longer want to use the distancing, dualistic language of otherness. Instead I want to look within the Christian tradition for ways to affirm the key importance of difference while sharing in God's hospitality and welcome for all people and for the whole creation.

In order to articulate a hermeneutic of hospitality, we first need to understand postcolonial analysis, and feminist postcolonial analysis specifically. I will briefly outline postcolonial interpretation, how feminism fits within that analysis, and finally provide a theological example of how we could apply feminist postcolonial analysis. Using the doctrine of election, we can see how postcolonial feminist analysis works, through examining new ways of reading Scripture and exploring a foundation for a hermeneutic of hospitality.

POSTCOLONIAL INTERPRETATION

Postcolonial interpretation has been a developing field since 1978 and the publication of Edward Said's book *Orientalism.* Said focused on "colonial discourse—the variety of textual forms in which the West produced and codified knowledge about nonmetropolitan areas and cultures, especially those under colonial control."[2] The term "postcolonial" has many meanings, which are themselves contested, but I am using it in this book to denote not only a temporal period after colonization or a political transfer of power, but a strategy for analysis that unmasks colonial epistemological frameworks.[3] The work of postcolonial interpretation is both that of *analysis* and that of *resistance* and *reconstruction*, as scholars examine the many contradictions between the colonial and neocolonial rhetoric and the continuing cultural, political, economic, and religious oppression experienced by colonized peoples.[4] A postcolonial perspective examines all aspects of the colonial process from the beginning of colonial contact up to and including its present effects in both colonizing and colonized nations. It helps us acknowledge ways in which white, Euro-American colonialism and imperialism have helped to structure the world in terms of those who "have" and those who "need." Postcolonial theorists are committed to documenting the contradictions in their many fields, and to a future in which "post" applies not only to the centuries after colonial contact and struggles for independence, but also to a time after colonialism and imperialism are ended. Attention to rhetoric and literary theory has led biblical scholars to include these perspectives in their postmodern interpretations, and gradually scholars of religion have begun to write in this field.

Because of my history, I am surprised neither by calls today for *postcolonial* analysis from persons from the Global South, nor by persons from the North who are trying to view the colonial past and its resultant categorization of people into degrees of "otherness" with new eyes. When I see expressions of pain, frustration, and anger in the face of the continuing domination of people in countries of the South by those of us whose roots are in the cultures of the dominant nations of the North, I know a new way of thinking is necessary. I have chosen in this book to talk about ourselves as *postcolonial subjects*, because we all share a commonality through the colonial experience. Whether colonizer or colonized, we are all postcolonial subjects continually affected by the history and ongoing economic, religious, cultural, and political implications of colonialism, albeit in very different ways. Some countries were conquered in the name of religion, others for their gold, and some for political gain. I will ask how we can move away from the dualistic paradigm of oppressor/oppressed and look at ways that many different people can join in addressing all the death-dealing issues of injustice that are definitely not *post!*

Postcolonial perspectives are important for theologians in every part of the globe, be they part of the "Two-Thirds World" of the Southern Hemisphere or of the "One-Third World" of the Northern Hemisphere. Our religious and cultural histories are mixed together in our ever-changing worlds as these histories, or received stories of our past, continue to be challenged by global capitalism and modern technology. As postcolonial subjects, that is, all those who have been affected by the colonialist activities of the past, we share our groaning and unjust world together, and are sometimes both "colonizer" and "colonized" at the same time.

Postcolonial Subjects

To understand the challenges of postcolonial theory, we must first look at postcolonial analysis and how we are all implicated as postcolonial subjects. The important matter to note here is that neither party in this dialogue is solely colonizer or colonized. Of particular help in clarifying postcolonial analysis is the work of Musa Dube, a senior lecturer of New Testament at the University of Botswana, who challenges us to look at imperialist perspectives in the biblical tradition and particularly in the New Testament. Dube writes:

> The word *postcolonial* has been coined to describe the modern history of imperialism, beginning with the process of colonialism, through the struggles for political independence, the attainment of independence, and to the contemporary neocolonialist realities.[5]

She argues that colonialism has not ended but has only changed form, from physical occupation and government leadership in colonial times to the creation of an International Monetary Fund and a trade structure benefiting multinational corporations today. More specifically, postcolonial scholars are also concerned with what many people call the *American Empire,* that is, the global political, economic, and cultural domination by the United States, which affects the way people of all cultures and nations live within the United States as well as in other countries.

The modern history of imperialism shows us the interconnectedness of gender, economic, and political oppression. As *postcolonial subjects,* we are often simultaneously colonizers and colonized; it is necessary for us to analyze critically the sources and practices of privilege, but also to look for liberating spaces in which we can share our commitment to work against both international oppression and gendered oppression.[6]

One historical example of the link between gender and economic oppression involves clothing. In Ghana, wives of European missionaries taught the women to sew in order for them to cover their bodies in nineteenth-century garments, because the missionaries did not approve of the Ghanaian's traditional dress. The puffy sleeves of this era are still evident in Ghanian dress today. The women of Ghana were then dependent upon the missionaries for cloth and for sewing machines. At times feminists, particularly Euro-American feminists, direct their attention only toward patriarchy, neglecting the cultural, political, and socioeconomic factors involved. Yet in so doing, they ignore or fail to notice the resulting linguistic, cultural, political, and economic forms of domination that are included in the hierarchical structures and thought patterns of patriarchy—which is not a singular form of oppression.

These forces of language and cultural domination enable the international political and cultural structures of control and manipulation used against what Dube calls the Two-Thirds World, the majority of the world whose people are oppressed. Dube challenges postcolonial feminists to join in resisting all forms of imperialism. She understands imperialism to be a structural imposition of a few standards on a universal scale that assumes the "other" is a blank slate to be (1) inscribed with a universal (Western) culture in disregard of their own particular culture, and (2) rendered dependent on those who maintain these standards.[7]

In some instances, a powerful person within a colonized nation can recognize the danger of colonialism and order changes to be made. Elizabeth Amoah, professor of religion at the University of Ghana in Accra, describes just such a situation in Ghana.

> Generally, the rationale behind the introduction of western education in West Africa by the missionaries was to produce a class of Africans who would help spread western civilization and western Christianity. Boarding schools were introduced by the Methodist missionary Thomas Birch Freeman, who is believed to have said that the rationale behind the establishment of the boarding schools was to separate young children from their families and culture so that eventually they would forget about their African identities. The courses taught were basically Bible and European centered. While the men were being taught to be future catechists and teachers of the bible the women were taught mostly by missionary wives to be ideal Christian wives for the African converts. The courses that the African women were taught centered on domestic chores such as ironing, sewing, mending clothes, and cooking [mostly European food]. The colonizers' hope was that the Africans that went through the early missionary schools would not have the opportunity to learn anything about their continent and the lives of its citizens.
>
> In reaction to this, Kwame Nkrumah, the first head of state in Ghana, made it mandatory for the University of Ghana to introduce courses on African studies in its curriculum. He next asked the then Divinity School which was also established to train African missionaries and church workers, to widen its scope and to teach all the religions that reflected the religious pluralism in the country. Consequently, the Divinity School was changed to the Department for the Study of Religions, where courses in African indigenous religions and Islam were added to the existing curriculum.[8]

In postcolonial practice, the current power structures need to be reordered and responsive to colonized peoples reclaiming of their own traditions and redefinition of colonizing legacies.

Dube has proposed a strategy for working together as post-colonial subjects. She calls upon both the dominator and the dominated to examine the matrix of past and present imperialism and to map ways in which they can speak as equal subjects who meet to exchange words of wisdom and life.[9] The strategy is to examine imperialism *and* to map out ways to sit together. The strategy is a process with two components, but it has to be done in the sitting together of all parties. This is a tall order for us. Yet it is an agenda with which feminists are familiar. The critique of gender differences has long led us to seek out ways of cooperating to construct gender in a more egalitarian pattern, while allowing us also to recognize that we all remain entangled in a web of contradictions regarding gender. The same applies here as we seek to critique the effects of imperialism. We need to recognize and analyze both the impact of colonialism on our different social locations and our global interdependence. These are key aspects of the postcolonial feminist dialogue. The good news is that the dialogue is no longer just between "them and us," seated on opposite sides of the table, but with a postcolonial analysis we can now join together in a roundtable discussion.

Once we recognize ourselves as postcolonial subjects, the way we do theology will also change. From my point of view, post-colonial perspectives can both challenge and strengthen North American theologies as they reflect on God's welcoming and liberating presence in our lives and world. They do this by analyzing and resisting the ongoing effects of colonialism through imperialist practices on the colonized and the colonizers, and by joining God in re-creating a world that is life-giving for all women and children together with all men and the whole creation.

Postcolonial Theological Perspectives

A postcolonial theological perspective is only one of many that might be a source of insight into the liberating aspects of

difference, hospitality, and community. It is particularly helpful, however, as a guide *to the future*, because this perspective
recognizes that we are *all in a postcolonial situation* as both colonized and colonizing persons. We all bear the marks of colonial histories that have formed us. Listening with concern to
those who have paid the price of colonial expansion does not
mean that those whose nations have gained through this
process have nothing to say. Rather, it means that we are in this
together and need to sort out the power dynamics of our many
and various positions with care if we are to truly practice God's
hospitality with one another.

Everywhere, in each and every place, globalization makes us
all part of hybrid cultures; we must search out the meaning of
our identities, and work together across our differences to
bring justice and peace to a world that is divided.[10] I experienced a kind of hybridity in Sulawesi, Indonesia, in 2004.[11]
Shannon Clarkson and I went with a student from the Theological Seminary of Eastern Indonesia in Makassar on what was
to be an interfaith exchange among students. When we three
arrived at a small house for the discussion, we found ourselves,
two older white women and a young Indonesian woman, with
ten young men from Lapar, a Muslim education group, sitting
together on the floor around a low round table. Lapar had, in
collaboration with the local Muslim boys' schools, developed a
program that trained teachers to respect differing religious
beliefs. The goal of the program was to overcome the hatred
and violence between Muslims and Christians in their area. To
my surprise, postcolonialism was the topic they wanted to talk
about, and it had been postcolonial analysis that had led them
to seek a better way of living together as Muslim and Christian
partners in their conflicted community. The students identified
across lines of difference, holding their postcolonial hybridity
as common, instead of allowing their differences to become
divisive. Had we thought that postcolonial concerns were con-
fined to the academy, as the language in some journals would
indicate, we were sorely wrong. These young men were excit-
edly discussing the success they were having in their antivio-

lence and antihatred program. Perhaps this postcolonial perspective can also become a way ahead for those of us in Western nations to become partners with women and men in all parts of the globalized world.

The concept of *difference* can be a tool for, or a weapon against, understanding one another. Difference is a weapon when it is used as a reason to downgrade, exclude, silence, or oppress. The "other" becomes an object of scorn as an inferior person, simply because of biological characteristics that don't meet the universal norm of, for example, whiteness, maleness, health, or affluence. This is known as "essentializing difference" and is practiced to mark a group as having no common nature with the "normal or neutral ones." The dominant groups reinforce the negative use of difference out of fear of losing their privilege, as well as their identity, whose value comes in viewing themselves over against the "other."[12]

From the perspective of colonial subjects and those declared to be less than full persons because of their race, gender, orientation, or nationality, difference, as a tool, is a positive indication of their own distinct identity, culture, language, and history. *Emancipatory difference* reclaims the definition of the group by the group. In other words, the meanings we attach to differences are given value, positive or negative. A group's self-naming, reclaiming of the power to name themselves, affirms diversity over and against calls for uniformity. The claiming of a culture's own difference as good allows its members to create positive value and meaning for their culture. This raises questions for the Christian tradition. How does that tradition honor the rainbow diversity of God's creation? And how is it part of the imperialism that essentializes difference?

Asian theologian Kwok Pui-lan, the author of *Postcolonial Imagination and Feminist Theology*, has pointed out at least four critical keys for those who want to understand how the Christian theological tradition has been shaped by colonizing countries of the North.[13] They are very helpful in our exploration of a postcolonial theological perspective on the practice of hospitality.

1. The codification of knowledge. The first key component of postcolonial analysis is its clarification of the connection between colonialism and the codification of knowledge of all kinds, including theology and biblical studies. The modern academy emerged in Europe in the nineteenth century, and with it came an understanding of theological method, colonial expansion, and the study of "native peoples," which continues today. Western scholars began to codify the languages, cultures, religions, and histories of the many different nations that they chose to call Asia or the Orient. At the same time these scholars developed scientific views of historical criticism and theological discourse that served to make normative the Western "worldview" and remain the standards of excellence in the academy and academic publishing, although they are historically and culturally limited to one phase of history in one part of the world.

To counter this approach, I tried at Yale Divinity School to move into the twenty-first century by having students write their own reflections on topics in the course Theology of Hospitality, so we could read them together. The goal of the exercise was to reflect on how difference was experienced by the students in their lives and to relate their critical analysis of that experience to biblical and theological themes. When I asked students to write on "difference," several of them reflected this old ethos of superiority at work in the seminary, with one woman commenting on the way students at YDS try to outdo one another—"posturing their intelligence," and putting others down. The student was a second-career person returning to higher education. She noted how difference is reinforced in the classroom through use of knowledge from books (often written by white, male authors) versus knowledge from lived experience. The assignment not only asked them to use a "lesser valued" source of knowledge—their own experience, but also asked them to reflect on how academically valued sources reinforce difference in oppressive ways.

2. Decolonizing the mind. Kwok suggests that "postcolonial intellectuals need to be vigilant about the deep-seated layers of colonialist patterns of thinking in the archaeological excavation of their minds."[14] If we do not examine the assumptions we carry with us, we inadvertently reinforce Western thinking as "correct" and "better"; this is an issue not just for those who have benefited from colonization, but for those who were colonized as well. The connection between colonialism and the Enlightenment in Europe resulted in what might be called "the colonization of the mind." It is not much of an exaggeration to say that every aspect of the lives of colonized peoples was written about by their colonizers, whose scientific study of the history of India, Indonesia, and other nations provided these colonizers with knowledge that helped them politically dominate the colonized people they were studying. This type of scholarship continues today, with, for example, experts on Sanskrit or the religious life of Hindus in Bali earning their degrees in Euro-American universities through the study of the "other"; the Internet is full of such studies on every imaginable topic. Cultural specificity is erased when Western description and classification become the norm for the culture under examination and the inhabitants of that culture then adapt to the description. Those receiving training in Euro-American contexts are taught Western methods and use interpretive lenses that begin with a hierarchy of values determined by those who benefited from colonial power. Those who are "studied" are taught what they "ought to be," so that the domination continues through this colonization of the mind. Both those from colonized nations and those from colonizing nations need to decolonize their minds in order to be able to relate to one another as subjects rather than subjects and objects.

The following is an example of a study of the "other." Several years ago, Mercy Amba Oduyoye from Ghana, organizer of the Circle of Concerned African Women Theologians, was contacted by a European woman asking permission to attend and present a paper at an upcoming Circle meeting in Kenya. Mercy responded that only women from Africa who were Circle members were invited and eligible to present papers. Later on, when the Circle members began arriving at the conference, they were greeted by the woman, who had positioned a sign-board at the entrance, welcoming them to the meeting. As they entered, she handed out questionnaires for them to supply information about their involvement in the Circle for her research project. Although Mercy and others refused, they found themselves profiled a number of years later in *Circle Thinking: African Women Theologians in Dialogue with the West.*[15] Mercy sent a letter to Cambridge University, the school which had granted Carrie Pemberton a doctorate for the dissertation on the Circle, listing the many inaccuracies, untruths, and omissions in the book. Pemberton later wrote to Mercy thanking her but adding that her basic thesis about the Circle was correct.

A counterexample, one of decolonization of the mind, again concerns the Circle of Concerned African Women Theologians. The Circle was established in the mid-1980s to assist African women theologians develop a forum in which to write about *themselves*—precisely what the previous example was working against. This initiative has now expanded, and the Circle cooperates with the Yale Divinity School Women's Initiative on HIV/AIDS in Africa. It is now possible for women at the doctoral level to be trained both in Africa and at Yale in methods for shifting the cultural and theological attitudes of members of their local churches to understand the causes of HIV/AIDS and working toward eliminating false beliefs and practices that contribute to spreading the disease. The women from the Circle are able to use knowledge from their experience and training in Africa as well as Yale University. Each basis of knowledge serves as a check on the other to prevent reinforcing imperialist, Western views from dominating the religious response to HIV/AIDS in Africa.

3. Framework of mutually constituted oppressions. Oppressions are interrelated and reinforce each other. We may experience only one or two forms of oppression. However, as noted earlier, we cannot work to eradicate only one form of oppression—such as gender—without recognizing that economic and racial discrimination exacerbates gender oppression. Postcolonial analysis does not in itself remove the forms of oppression that people experience, but it provides a framework for understanding mutually constituted oppressions, which then allows us to recognize their socially constructed interconnections and respond theologically. With globalization it is no longer possible to focus on only one form of oppression, because they are all intertwined. Racism, classism, imperialism, and all the other "isms" are woven together, and many people are doubly or triply oppressed, so that people do not have access to what they need to survive, let alone flourish.

The chances for a poor, HIV-positive Ethiopian woman in Addis Ababa to earn a living are very slim, for the oppressions—sexism, racism, heterosexism, and classism—reinforce each other. Let me explain what I mean. There will be no solution to poverty or to HIV/AIDS unless we begin to eliminate the patriarchal structures of domination that collude with poverty to multiply the oppression of countless women and families. With regard to HIV/AIDS, faithful Christian women in southern Africa are admonished by their priests to submit to the authority and desires of their husbands, who often refuse to wear condoms and thus put their wives at risk for contracting HIV/AIDS or increasing their viral load, exacerbating their health problems. Without economic access outside of a marriage, many women are kept by poverty in patriarchal relationships that jeopardize their very lives. Nor will there be any solution to the hierarchy of racial or cultural differences without the recognition that how difference is constructed is itself a tool for oppression and manipulation, although differences themselves are a God-given gift. There will be no solution to ecological destruction without recognition of the structures of global capitalism that value profit more than people and their lands. "Identity politics"—*the idea that common identities are a source for political action*—around one issue is important, but ultimately the endeavor needs partnership to "make a difference," so that the differences are not essentialized and reinforced in a negative manner.

Postcolonialism calls us to adopt a more holistic interpretive perspective, that is, to interpret biblical and church tradition, not just from our own perspectives, but also by exploring how these traditions reinforce social structures of injustice. The positive impact of this kind of approach and its resulting shift in the way I do theology came home to me in 2002 at the Asian Regional Consultation of the WCC's study on Women's Voices and Visions of the Church in Seoul, Korea.[16] The thirty women participants, all of whom worked in theology and ministry, were very much focused on the hybridity, or mixture, of religions in their geographic region. Over and over they told of ways they had found to work with women of different religious and cultural groups against the political, economic, social, and personal violence that so characterizes their postcolonial situations. In the process, they incorporated new forms of spirituality and worship outside the church, in small streets, and in the public square to confront the combined structures of injustice in their lives. A Sri Lankan woman told of an art project of street murals created by the Dalit people, formerly called "untouchables," that brought their community together but also included others outside their community who contributed their art as well. Leonila Bermisa of the Philippines spoke of multifaith and ecumenical gatherings of people who had joined together for the transformation of their society.[17]

4. Focus on North American imperialism. Postcolonial writing and analysis is particularly focused on what Salman Rushdie speaks of as the empire writing back to the center, that is, a claiming of the power to narrate, to contest, and to reconstruct meanings. But postcolonial analysis does not stop with the biblical empires or nineteenth-century empires. As I have said, it is concerned with what many people call the American imperialism, that is, the global political, economic, and cultural domination of the United States, which affects the way people of all cultures and nations live within the United States as well as in other countries.

We in the United States need to be aware of the global impact of American foreign policy on the lives of students, faculty, and church members who make up the theological educational institutions around the world. To be relevant, theological/seminary curricula need to be grounded in a continuing search for justice that can enable theological educators to talk back to empire, as theological educators and their students outside the United States create their own forms of theological education.

After being asked in 1986 to teach in the Doctorate of Ministry program of Presbyterian San Francisco Theological Seminary (SFTS) the following summer, I asked if I could invite a cohort of international feminists. With permission granted, I sought out the editor of *In God's Image*, the journal of Asian women theologians, the coordinator of the Ecumenical Association of Third World Theologians, a Minjung pastor in Korea, a feminist teacher in Japan, and a few others to join me that summer. As that group graduated, enthusiasm about the program had surfaced and Hisako Kinukawa of Japan and Chung Sook-Ja of Korea met with the SFTS DMin director, Walt Davis, Shannon Clarkson, and myself, at the 1992 AAR/SBL meeting in San Francisco. We determined to begin an International Feminist DMin the following summer in Tokyo, Japan, to be coordinated by Asian women in Japan and Korea.

Certain guidelines were created early on in the program: the focus is on women in countries of the Global South; participants do not need to be ordained; the program is open to Roman Catholics and others; scholarship assistance is available to those admitted from the South, though they are encouraged to seek aid from their denominations or elsewhere.

Over the course of the program, the state of feminist consciousness has changed. Originally we were introducing feminist ideas, or rather giving names to concepts the women were struggling with in their situations. Now they come fairly well versed in the literature and familiar, as well, with the dangers of life as a feminist. Their papers reflect a social analysis of their context as well as the theological climate. The focus is on their location and their ability to speak back to empire. The books chosen for those reflections are representative of a geographical range of feminist thought. We have determined that program participation, whether or not the thesis is completed, changes perspectives. Living together in those two-week sessions creates memories, a much broader concern for citizens of the world, and a new confidence about feminist theology, ethics, and interpretation of the Bible, and the six-week summer session creates strong bonds. Most importantly, studying as a group provides the courage needed in many countries to continue working for justice for women in the midst of patriarchal social structures that frequently condemn what they accomplish. Such programs are an example of contexts in which postcolonial theology is being done.

THE DOCTRINE OF ELECTION
IN POSTCOLONIAL INTERPRETATION

Over the years various theological traditions along with certain biblical texts, have been used in service of colonialism and today can continue to perpetuate imperial practices. The doctrine of election is a theological example of ways in which the Christian tradition has decided to use "difference" as a means of oppressing people. I will use the doctrine of election to provide an example of postcolonial analysis and a revisioning of hospitality. The issue of election—who is in or chosen and who is out—has been used historically to exclude and divide, rather than as God's mandate for radical hospitality. The divisions of chosenness have often served religiously, politically, racially, gendered, and economically dominant groups. However, when using a hermeneutic of hospitality builds on the insights of postcolonial thought, the doctrine of election can become a call to include outsiders and open God's welcome to all.

If we are to find our way to new structures of interdependence as postcolonial feminist Christians, we need to work critically with our Christian theological and biblical traditions. There is a deep ambiguity in the foundational stories of divine liberation in the Jewish and Christian traditions that, for Christians, leads into the Christian doctrine of election. Unfortunately amid the intolerance and religious fundamentalism with which we are so familiar today, many of us have forgotten Judith Plaskow's insight, that "it is not in the chosenness that cuts off, but in the distinctiveness that opens itself to difference that we find the God of Israel and of each and every people."[18] The traditional interpretations of divine liberation, leading into Christian understandings of election have, however, not focused on inclusivity of *each and every people* as part of God's intention.

When Election Is a Problem

The Christian tradition begins its claim to election with the covenant stories in the Hebrew Scriptures. However, from a postcolonial perspective, the covenant story of deliverance in Exodus and the story of conquest in Joshua are problematic. The land of Canaan is promised both to Abraham and his descendants and to Moses, even though that land is already occupied by other groups of people (Gen. 15:18–21; Exod. 3:17) and must be invaded: "and when the LORD your God gives them over to you and you defeat them, then you must utterly destroy them" (Deut. 7:2).[19] Christians, claiming the superior revelation of God's redemption, carried this story of chosenness in Deuteronomy 7:2–9 forward, as Christ's universal messianic mandate to them. Here God says they were chosen simply because God loved them, not because they had special qualities.

You might imagine that indigenous people read this text and wonder what God has in store for them. Native Americans read this text and identify with the Canaanites. Robert Warrior, member of the Osage Nation, writes:

No matter what we do, the conquest narratives will remain. As long as people believe in the Yahweh of deliverance, the world will not be safe from Yahweh the conqueror. But perhaps, if they are true to their struggle, people will be able to

achieve what Yahweh's chosen people in the past have not: a
society of people delivered from oppression who are not so
afraid of becoming victims again that they become oppressors
themselves, a society where the original inhabitants can
become something other than subjects to be converted to a
better way of life.[20]

In Deuteronomy chosenness and the gift of land are thus
accomplished by taking, conquering a land that belonged to
others; thus the oppressed become the oppressor.

Similarly, Christian claims to universalism and the attitudes
that led the colonists to claim for themselves the land they had
discovered, Rosemary Radford Ruether argues, "were shaped
culturally within the Greco-Roman Empire, which believed
itself to be a universal empire containing the one true human-
istic culture."[21] In order to be considered human, people had
to assimilate into that culture. Those who didn't were called
barbarians.

This combination of messianic universalism and Greco-
Roman imperialist universalism provided early Christians with
a mandate for mission. This perceived mandate was, in turn,
the inspiration behind the nineteenth-century partnership
between Christianity and European imperialism that wiped
out others' cultures, religions, and political systems to establish
uniformity through enforcement of Christianity and new economic systems. Christian missionary calls provided the justification for creating uniformity that financially benefited the
colonizers. To be counted as "one of the elect," colonized people were forced to assimilate, to be *saved* from their savage ways
of living. Colonizers manipulated theological language to reinforce practices of conquest. The legacy of this imperialism is
still with us today in the actions of the United States in
Afghanistan, as it carries out what President George W. Bush
first called "Operation Infinite Justice" and then renamed
"Operation Enduring Freedom," appropriating Christian theological language to describe and elicit support for the U.S.
invasion in the Middle East. The former was changed within

weeks of its inception on 9/11, after Muslim groups objected, saying only Allah could provide "infinite justice."

The Ambiguity of Chosenness

The Christian doctrine of election, which carries with it an understanding of chosenness for some, has helped to reinforce this historic behavior. Time and again in the Bible the oppressed become the oppressors. The story of the Syrophoenician woman in Mark 7 illustrates that the doctrine of election is situation variable. The meaning of election changes over time in the world and in the Gospels. Jesus' mind is changed by a woman who is an outsider, who asks him to realize a new perspective on chosenness and exclusion. Broadening the problem further, Renita Weems has linked race and election, and argued that a womanist perspective must criticize theological assumptions and biases found in the Bible by beginning with an analysis of election:

> The Bible's renown, I believe, is grounded in large part in the claim of Israel's (and later the Church's) election. Therefore, to identify the biblical world as patriarchal . . . is only to talk about symptoms. Those who have been excluded from Judeo-Christian theological discourse and structures must begin their work with an analysis of "election."[22]

Election, for Weems, is a primary theological source used by those in power to divide on racial and gender lines, determining who is fit and unfit, who is worthy and unworthy.

The understanding of election in the Bible itself is frequently both ambiguous and contradictory. On the one hand, to be chosen by God is to be chosen as a *partner* in the care of the earth and of all God's creatures. At the same time, however, to be chosen as a king or as a special people is to be chosen to exercise *dominion* over those not so favored by God. In the Bible we discover over and over a cycle of the deformation of the idea of election, as election with a goal of survival and service turns into election for security and superiority. The idea of

Israel as a unique people chosen by God is critiqued by the prophet Amos (9:7), who is criticizing the understanding of election as privilege, and in later writings such as the story of Ruth and in Jonah 4:9–11.[23] Ruth, the outsider, becomes the ancestor of King David, and Boaz, her husband, becomes a model of hospitality to the foreigner and widow, which is in direct contradiction of the earlier Israelite view that foreign wives should be excluded from Israel. Jonah, when asked by God to save the city of Nineveh refuses to share the message of love with them. But the persistent criticism of the exploitation of election for personal or national gain did not change Israel's belief that the people of Israel were a special part of God's plan for the whole world.[24]

It is not surprising that this attitude continues in the New Testament. Both the Gospels and Paul struggle with whether the teaching of Jesus about welcome into God's household (exemplified in Luke 4:18–19 with the calling to the oppressed, in Matthew 22:1–14 with the invitation to all the outsiders to the welcome banquet, and in Galatians 2:1–10, where we read Paul's commission to spread the gospel to all the world) is only for the Jews or for all people. Mark 7:24–30, the story of the Syrophoenician woman, portrays Jesus himself as needing to be taught by the woman that it is possible for him to heal those who are not God's children.[25]

FEMINISM AND HOSPITALITY
IN POSTCOLONIAL INTERPRETATION

The recent critiques by postcolonial scholars of the biblical message of election, along with its contemporary influences of messianic and imperialistic universalism, challenge us all to search out ways that patriarchal and imperial paradigms are constantly at work in biblical and church tradition and in the culture. I believe that adopting a postcolonial feminist analysis in the development of a hermeneutic of hospitality can help us in this effort. First, postcolonial feminist analysis helps us to, as Mary Ann Tolbert has said, "recognize the legitimacy of self-consciously adopting different perspectives on a text at different times."[26] There is no one universal meaning of a text or tradition; they are all subject to continuing discussion of our many local readings that vary with time, space, and culture. Second, postcolonial feminist interpretations are a critical tool for transforming Christian traditions in ways that may be life giving to those who share in the struggles of colonized and oppressed peoples. Third, these interpretations invite us into a discussion of how to move toward interdependence in our traditions as well as our actions, by acknowledging ourselves to be postcolonial subjects who are caught in the web of global destruction.

These aspects of postcolonial feminist interpretation evidence new ways to respond to God's invitation to be partners in the mending of creation. With this foundation for a hermeneutic of hospitality, we can do no less than search for ways that the traditions make sense of our lives and faith. We can do so without being destructive of other peoples.

A Feminist Hermeneutic of Hospitality

Election is not the only Christian tradition that describes how people of the covenant should relate to their neighbors. Another important tradition in this respect is hospitality. In facing the challenge of a world of abundant difference and more than abundant experiences of exclusion and suffering, often rooted in a disdain for the "other," a feminist hermeneutic of hospitality can make it clear that in God's sight no one is "other." In this regard there are at least three ways we can begin resisting deformation of the doctrine of election. Our hermeneutic of hospitality can (1) pay attention to the *power quotient* involved in what is said and who is saying it, (2) give priority to the *perspective of the outsider*, and (3) rejoice in *God's unfolding promise*. Let me explain what I mean.

1. Paying attention to the power quotient. People have varied levels of power and access based on their social location. The way in which we choose to use our power can bring the power quotient into balance through sharing of power. The doctrine of election, like other interpretations of Christian traditions, is socially constructed. That is, its meaning changes over time and in different social, political, and economic contexts. One important factor in how we read and interpret the meaning of God's calling in persons' lives is the power quotient that exists among and in the relationships of the groups involved. The idea of election as a sign of God's special care has historically fulfilled a need among the powerless for identity as human beings. Those who were viewed as "nobody" could affirm their own self-worth and their *inclusion* as children of God granted full human dignity and worth as a gift of God's love. No wonder not only the tribes of Israel and the nobodies of the early church, but also those in every culture who have been considered less than human, have found in election the strength to resist many different forms of oppression. A problem arises, however, when a people who consider themselves special in the eyes of God use their power and privilege to dominate others, for then this inclusive and empowering understanding of election is deformed, and election becomes a hierarchy of orthodoxy and exclusion.

A feminist postcolonial interpretation would make it clear that this deformed understanding of election provided divine reinforcement for the ideas and practices of racism and imperialist expansion in the United States, South Africa, and elsewhere. It would also lead us to ask about the power quotient in texts such as Luke 14:7–14, the parable of the Wedding Banquet, in which persons are asked to take the lower seat in humility, and to invite the poor to their banquets, not just friends who can repay the invitation. New Testament scholar Sharon Ringe, writing in *The Postcolonial Bible*, has observed that in the United States we can use a postcolonial reading to look at the text and see that the elite groups, like the leader of the Pharisees who invited Jesus for a meal, are being enjoined to humility and generosity.[27] She could check the guest list for those who are missing. She could ask, Where are the women in the story? Would they count as "poor, crippled, lame, and blind"? What if those who are excluded decided to have a meal on their own instead of being brought in? In our churches today, as in the parable, the guest list and the seating arrangement are determined by those in power. Surely the table that we long for would find a way to include all who would share the power *so that the power quotient would be balanced.*

In 2002, Mercy Oduyoye, Elizabeth Amoah, Rabiatu Ammah, my partner, Shannon Clarkson, and I taught at the Institute of Women in Religion and Culture, in Accra, Ghana. We worked together on issues of gospel and culture as a group of fifteen women (ten students, five teachers) from nine different countries as part of the international feminist Doctor of Ministry program sponsored by San Francisco Theological Seminary (SFTS) and the World Council of Churches (WCC) that I mentioned earlier.[28] The power quotient was always at the center of our dialogue, because a major purpose of this doctoral program is to empower women from countries of the South as they become leaders in their communities and therefore subjects of their own theology and history. One goal is to equip these women with the necessary resources and educational tools to write theology in English as part of this empowerment, because the seminary requires us to do so. We know that this means we are also perpetuating the imperialism of the English language and Western educational standards. However, because those in power determine "who sits at the table," a way to bring more international women to the table is to use our own privilege as Western educators to teach them theology in English, while holding up as a valid source of theology their experiences—not just the English books they read.

2. Giving priority to the perspective of the outsider. In the history of the church, election has also pointed to the church's calling to witness and service, and biblical and church tradition have emphasized these tasks for which the community has been chosen. But witness and service have been deformed by an assumption that those who share the gospel and bring Christ have an elevated role that makes them superior to others.

A postcolonial feminist reconstruction of election would have us ask what our calling to service means by *listening* to those on the margin, who will define their need and teach us the meaning of God's welcome and hospitality. Referring back to the banquet text of Luke 14:7–14 just discussed, giving priority to the outsider would require, first, that they be on the guest list and, second, that they be consulted about the seating arrangements and food. This "preferential option for the outsider" is another way of saying what Latin American liberation theologians call God's "preferential option for the poor." It is not an exclusive option, but rather a starting point for giving attention to and working toward overcoming injustice.[29]

When we begin from the outsider's perspective, we develop the practice of listening to the pain of others and responding to their initiatives. Yet when we try to begin from the perspective of another, we must remind ourselves that we cannot really "walk in another's moccasins." We can never fully grasp the perspective of someone from another culture, nor can they fully understand the perspective of a colonizer. But this need not stop us from hearing and listening and working together. Iris Marion Young, professor of public and international affairs at the University of Pittsburgh, writes:

> Participants in communicative interaction are in a relation of approach. They meet across distances of time and space and can touch, share, overlap their interests. But each brings to the relationships a history and structured positioning that makes them different from one another, with their own shape, trajectory, and configuration of forces.[30]

Young says that listening is hearing and heeding the call to be just in our concrete social and political practices.[31] No call is so clear today as the call from countries in Africa concerning the pandemic of HIV/AIDS. One small response in which I have been engaged is the joint project I discussed between the Circle of Concerned African Women Theologians and the YDS Women's Initiative on HIV/AIDS.[32] In this program, African and American theologians work together to transform the traditional theologies and ethics of sexuality, which have contributed to sexist and heterosexist doctrines. The theologies and ethics of sexuality were developed by Euro-American male theologians and were exported to Africa in the process of colonization and missionization. Many of the behaviors supported by Christian sexual ethics, in particular, place women at risk for HIV/AIDS—such as women being subservient to their husbands (for childbearing or sexual intercourse) even when the husband is aware of his HIV-positive status. The program supports women in African faith-based communities who are struggling to find ways to provide AIDS education, prevention, and care that attends directly to the needs of women and children and the oppression they face.

3. **Recognizing and rejoicing in God's unfolding promise.** As we use a hermeneutic of hospitality, one other guard against the deformation of election by those who think there is only one answer to the meaning of God's calling—and they have it—is to recognize that God's promise is a promise and not a guarantee. It is *a promise that keeps unfolding* in new ways in our lives and in lives that are so very different from our own. The unfolding nature of God's promise of justice and love serves as a safeguard against the misuse of religious practices to "guarantee" that we are chosen, and changes our understanding of election as new challenges to the meaning of God's promises become clear to us.

For example, let us return to the story of the nameless Syrophoenician woman. The story appears in both Mark 7:24–30 and Matthew 15:21–28, although there are differences between the two.[33] This text has had many feminist interpretations because it goes beyond the emphasis on Gentile mission and is focused on a woman who talks Jesus into expanding his mission beyond the people of Israel.[34] Mark presents the Syrophoenician or Greek woman as assertive, articulate, and willing to find Jesus and confront him in order to heal her daughter. Matthew's version, however, seems to incorporate a deformation of the idea of election: all people are to be welcomed, but *not all are to be of equal worth*. The woman is now demoted to the status of Canaanite, with a daughter "tormented by a demon," evoking with this memories of the first conquest of the Canaanites and their demonic worship of "false gods." The woman is so clearly *other* that Jesus even calls her a "dog" rather than a child of God. This form of election leaves the "other" out, and at the very least it must be challenged, as the woman challenges Jesus to open up the promise to all people without requiring them to become people of God.

Perhaps such an unfolding of God's welcome will help us move beyond the hermeneutic of the "other" and toward a more inclusive hermeneutic of hospitality. A project known as "A Shared Garden" demonstrates the truth that empowerment can come from recognizing that *God's promise is always unfolding*. A Shared Garden is the creation of women from Brazil, Chile, and the United States who came together to create an opportunity for ecofeminist encounter and dialogue focused on issues of religion and violence. Mary E. Hunt and Diann Neu from the Women's Alliance for Ethics and Ritual (WATER) in Silver Spring, Maryland, joined Ivone Gebara from Recife, Brazil, and the collective of Con-Spirando from Santiago, Chile, for three meetings in 1997 and 1998. At each meeting participants came from both continents and beyond, spending ten days together in seminar and discussion, prayer and ritual, excursions and workshops. The goal was to develop strategies for coping with violence in their respective settings, strategies that would overlap and reinforce one another. The meetings were led by this international team and colleagues local to each area. More than eighty women participated in all.

This Shared Garden for women in South, Central, and North America created a network throughout the Americas among women theologians, pastors, and community workers to do theology. The women, focusing on ecofeminist theological insights as well as practical experiences of religiously sanctioned violence, using their imaginations as well as their analytic skills, transformed their individual experiences into a new collective wisdom. Describing the event in Chile, Ivone Gebara said:

> We must go beyond the separations that come from economics. . . . We know we must keep our own cultures, our specific problems, the taste of our own food. Not everything has to be McDonald and Coca Cola. But we have [begun] to share an experience together of something very rich and good.[35]

This kind of experience of hospitality can act as an invitation to us all to join together in imagining a different world, one like a shared garden where all are welcome. Recognizing that God's knowledge is always unfolding is our invitation to work together as postcolonial subjects to find the many ways we can keep faith with our sisters and brothers as well as with a God who knows no partiality. In the face of overwhelming global challenges, such efforts cannot claim to change the world, but we can "keep on keeping on," hoping that Gustavo Gutiérrez was right in his final remark at the Denver meeting I mentioned at the beginning of this chapter, when he said that we need an additional Beatitude in the Sermon on the Mount (Matt. 5:1–12). We need to add, *Blessed are the obstinate and stubborn*; those who refuse to stop trying to make the world postracist, postcolonial, and more like the one for which God longs.

Postcolonial Subjects Practicing Hospitality

Practicing hospitality as postcolonial subjects *runs the risk* of deformation of intention and domination. But as we move from "other" to "partner," the give-and-take of hospitality makes it possible for power to be shared rather than used to dominate. The *hybridity,* or mix, of the familial, cultural, political, and economic contexts, in which each of us lives out roles simultaneously as a member of both colonizer and colonized groups, challenges us to listen with new ears to the cries of pain and hope that are offered by our brothers and sisters, and to join them in imagining a different way of relationship that points to God's intention to mend the whole of creation, beginning with ourselves.

The question for us as we seek to practice hospitality as post-colonial subjects is, how can we join our sisters and their brothers in such struggles against imperial and gendered oppression? Each of us can address the question in our writing, teaching, and ministries by reasserting difference as a crucial part of justice and the overcoming of oppression and domination. This is a "tall order," but ours is a world where we can no longer talk of unity under one truth or under one dominant superpower. Today, God's hospitality as a partnership with humankind in the "repair of the world" becomes the mandate as we look for ways to work with one another to transform the world.

In response to the old strategies of domination, postcolonial strategies honor the need to develop cultural identity as well as the need for identity politics. But these strategies go further than this. They recognize that a globalized society calls for the recognition of our common colonial histories as colonizers, collaborators, and colonized, and calls us to join across differences in our common work of sharing in God's creation.

This perspective is not a simple or easy response to our world of difference and danger, but it does provide a common set of tools for *analysis, resistance, and reconstruction* that have been forged by people coming from formerly colonized nations, the ones those in the North so often think of as "other." In God's New Creation the margins will no longer exist, for all will be part of the family. But until then, we can follow Jesus' advice and look to the margin as we seek out ways of practicing God's hospitality and praying with those of the Ninth Assembly of the WCC, *God in your grace transform the world! . . . Beginning with us!*

Questions for Thought

1. In what ways and at what times do you most often recognize your postcolonial location? What is your response when you recognize it?

2. What legacy do you, your faith community, and/or your country of citizenship inherit from colonial systems? (See Musa Dube, note 33.)
3. Can you find historical examples in your church tradition that demonstrate exclusionary practices that might be grounded in the doctrine of election?
4. Similar to liberation theologies' "preferential option for the poor," what is the starting point from which you work to overcome injustice? What is your motivating reason to overcome injustice?
5. Give an example of a person who might represent or demonstrate the phrase "blessed are the obstinate and stubborn." Have you ever found yourself acting this way?

3

Riotous Difference as God's Gift to the Church

I wish I could share all the love in my heart,
remove all the bars that still keep us apart.
I wish you could know what it means to be me,
then you'd see and agree everyone should be free.[1]

Throughout the previous chapter, we discovered how differences are deeper and more diverse than if we simply look at categories of identity such as male or female, black or white, colonizer or colonized. In this chapter, I want to look at biblical accounts that inform how we understand difference as part of God's intention and our call to create unity out of, not in spite of, that difference. How will unity ever be achieved through exclusion or domination based on differences? Unity in hospitality provides an alternative to current forms of unity, such as unity in tension. I suggest that hospitality is the practice of God's welcome by reaching out across difference to participate in God's actions bringing justice and healing in our world of crisis and our fear of the ones we call "other."

BIBLICAL VIEWS OF DIFFERENCE

It seems to me that God just does not like uniformity in human life and community or in nature. It seems that God's intention is to "remove all the bars" and create *a world full of riotous difference.* The writers of the biblical story of creation in Genesis describe just such a world. Each time God creates life of another kind, there is the refrain: "And God saw that it was good" (Gen. 1:25). At the end of the creation story God even saw that it was *very* good! But, as we know, as the biblical story moves on toward building towers, differences become part of the problem of sin. Perhaps if we analyze the problem of our inability or fear of difference, we can see more clearly how to embrace difference as a gift of God.

The New Testament telling of Pentecost offers clues to another way of responding to difference. However, before we reflect on why God's pentecostal gift of understanding in Acts 2 is so important we need to go back and look at the story of the tower of Babel in Genesis 11, which tells of the advent of misunderstanding at the dawn of human history.

Babel's Gift of Difference

Now the whole earth had one language and the same words. And as they migrated from the east, they came upon a plain in the land of Shinar and settled there. And they said to one another, "Come, let us make bricks, and burn them thoroughly." And they had brick for stone, and bitumen for mortar. Then they said, "Come, let us build ourselves a city, and a tower with its top in the heavens, and let us make a name for ourselves; otherwise we shall be scattered abroad upon the face of the whole earth." The LORD came down to see the city and the tower, which mortals had built. And the LORD said, "Look, they are one people, and they have all one language; and this is only the beginning of what they will do; nothing that they propose to do will now be impossible for them. Come, let us go down, and confuse their language there, so that they will not understand one another's speech." So the LORD scattered them abroad from there over the face of all the earth, and they left off building the city. Therefore it was called Babel, because there the LORD confused the language of all the earth; and from there the LORD scattered them abroad over the face of all the earth. (Gen. 11:1–9)

The story of the tower of Babel in Genesis 11:1–9 is part of the prologue to the call of Sarah and Abraham in Genesis 12. This prologue describes the way in which the biblical authors experience alienation and sin in their world.[2] Their account of the fall of the nations, with the resulting confusion of their language and their dispersal across the earth, points toward God's efforts to limit the results of sin. The structures of society are no longer benefiting the people but harming them. The people have begun to compete with God, creating a large city with a tower to proclaim their power. As a consequence God shatters their power, and the people are scattered "abroad over the face of all the earth" (Gen. 11:9). As theologian José Miguez Bonino notes, God's action is twofold: the thwarting of the project of the false unity of domination *and* the liberation of the nations that possess their own races, languages, and families.[3]

In the Babel story the scattering of peoples and the confusion of language are God's response to those who seek to triumph over others by means of domination. In building their tower to heaven they tried to consolidate their power and become like God, controlling all the people by means of a single language and political structure. Although the word "Babel" means *confuse* in Hebrew, the name Babel evoked in the biblical hearers' minds the dominating power of the Babylonian empire and its goal of securing unity through enforced uniformity. In today's Iraq, Babylon is a suburb of Baghdad, once again the site of fierce fighting and destruction[4] over difference, and the sinning continues with each tribe trying to control the others. We, like the tower builders, continue to struggle with difference—differences of race, ethnicity, gender, age, and so on.

God's response to the tower builders' pride and lust for power is, once more, to create the *gift of difference!* Differences of race, gender, sexual orientation, language, or culture are not problems to be resolved and controlled by a dominant group. Rather they are important ways of assuring that God's gift of riotous diversity in all creation will continue. In fact, these differences are *gifts in themselves.* God's gift lets new voices be heard and languages and cultures flourish. This message of the importance of diversity is doubly important for us today as we watch the growing domination of the world by North American imperialism and one economic system, and by a growing requirement that people learn English in order to be included in the global economic outreach of the United States.

The ecumenical movement is one place where the impact of "tower building" can be addressed. On November 28, 1998, the second day of the World Council of Churches Decade Festival of Churches in Solidarity with Women in Harare, Zimbabwe, women from all over the world processed to the stage with containers of water from their regions and poured it into a large jug. The pentecostal Spirit of God was truly present in Harare as the women celebrated the presence of God's Spirit in their midst, bringing them together across great differences of language, nationality, church affiliation, and economic and political location. The water symbolized the source of life as well as the tears of women's pain as they struggle for life in the midst of so much death-dealing war, poverty, violence, and oppression. In the meeting there was an outpouring of the Holy Spirit as women came together to share ways God's Spirit had been "troubling the waters," bringing forth New Creation and transformation in the lives of women in the churches (Gen. 1:1–2).[5] Such an outpouring of unity in the midst of great diversity gave us renewed confidence that the Spirit makes it possible to understand one another across our differences.[6]

Opposition to tower building by the powerful was very much on the agenda of the Eighth Assembly of the WCC in Harare in 1998 as it voted on two new statements, one on the debt crisis and one on human rights. The WCC has long had a policy on human rights, which has been reviewed and renewed at the last three assemblies. But having a policy and witnessing its implementation are two different things, so this new one called particularly for the "churches to overcome exclusion and marginalization in their own midst and to provide for full participation in their lives and governance."[7] In addition, the severely threatened because of exorbitant interest rates on loans from the International Monetary Fund, the World Bank, and other lenders. In his comments to the press about the jubilee call, the Rev. Dr. Konrad Raiser, then WCC General Secretary, said that while the WCC "is not an organization to put pressure on or propose conditions to governments," he hopes the process will "include a search for a new ethical borrowing and lending mechanism."[10]

For both issues, the struggle was to find ways to block the domination of one group over others so that everyone might have room to live as free daughters and sons of God. On the issue of debt, there was agreement to call for debt relief and an end to efforts to build the "tower" of the new economic order. But on the issue of human rights, there was no agreement about including anything on the subject of the rights of gays and lesbians and so construction of the "tower" of heterosexism continued. In response, Paul Sherry, who was then president of the United Church of Christ in the United States, said,

> I am saddened that the statement does not more sharply specify those whose basic human rights are severely threatened, particularly gay and lesbian people. . . . I understand and respect the differing theological postures on the appropriateness of homosexual orientation. But that is not the issue here. The issue is the protection of basic human rights for all God's children, without exception.[11]

In the light of the Babel story, the concerns and conflicts generated by the human rights statement from the WCC, about whether the rights of homosexuals could be mentioned in the document, make clear that some tower building is still going on. The rights of the heterosexual majority take precedence over all others. Keeping peace in the family overtakes recognizing that some family members are not included in order to keep that peace. Those who are excluded are often subject to familial and societal violence. Their human rights need to be protected. When reading the story of Babel in conjunction with Acts 2, we see that unity comes, not through building a tower of domina-

declaration rejected attempts by any group to deny hun
rights "on the basis of culture, religion, tradition, special so<
economic or security interests."[8] There were many discussi<
seeking also to include the issue of homosexuality, but the p
gram committee asked instead that a study and dialogue
issues of human sexuality be created. Underlying this decisi
were numerous comments from the preconference festi\
marking the end of the Ecumenical Decade of Churches
Solidarity with Women. The preconference eventually reach<
consensus on the following statement:

> We recognize that there are a number of ethical and theo-
> logical issues such as abortion, divorce, human sexuality in
> all of its diversity, that have implications for participation,
> and are difficult to address in the church community. Dur-
> ing the decade we acknowledge that human sexuality in all
> of its diversity has emerged with particular significance. We
> condemn the violence perpetrated due to differences on this
> matter. We wrestled with this issue, aware of the anguish we
> all endure because of the potential to create further divi-
> sions. We acknowledge that there is divided opinion. . . . In
> fact, for some women and men in our midst, the issue has
> no legitimacy. We seek the wisdom and the guidance of the
> Holy Spirit that we may continue the conversation in order
> that justice may prevail.[9]

Unlike the policy on human rights, the call to end the deb
crisis received a more unanimous approval. Since the 1970s
the WCC has addressed the debt crisis. As the Harare Assem
bly was celebrating its fiftieth anniversary and thus its jubile
year, the call was made to work on ending the debt crisis ii
the spirit of the biblical jubilee traditions (Exod. 23:10–12
Isa. 61:1–2a; Lev. 25; Acts 4:34). The text of the proposal "5.2
The Debt Issue: A jubilee call to end the stranglehold o
debt on impoverished peoples" was approved at the Assembl\
with several revisions from the floor. In this case, th<
anti–tower building forces were in the majority as they sough
to seek debt cancellation for those nations whose viability wa

tion or uniformity, but through communication. Acts 2 does not say that the people no longer had their own languages and customs but that they could understand one another. Our calling to welcome others in Christ is no easy task. Sometimes, when we are faced with so many differences and so much pain, it seems like an impossible possibility! Although the church is one in Christ, it lives each day torn by difference and seeking to manifest that oneness. It also lives each day with the vision that one day God will fulfill the unity of the church and mend the creation that has been so torn apart. Then each of us will cease to live *apart* from one another and will become *a part* of God's beautifully diverse creation.

Pentecost's Gift of Understanding

When the day of Pentecost had come, they were all together in one place. . . . All of them were filled with the Holy Spirit and began to speak in other languages, as the Spirit gave them ability.

Now there were devout Jews from every nation under heaven living in Jerusalem. And at this sound the crowd gathered and was bewildered, because each one heard them speaking in the native language of each. Amazed and astonished, they asked, "Are not all these who are speaking Galileans? And how is it that we hear, each of us, in our own native language?" . . .

In the last days it will be, God declares,
that I will pour out my Spirit upon all flesh,
    and your sons and your daughters shall prophesy,
and your young men shall see visions,
    and your old men shall dream dreams.
                                    (Acts 2:1, 4–8, 17)

The story of Pentecost in Acts 2:1–21 has often been understood as a sign of the reversal of Babel's message of diversity: now nations are brought together and united in the outpouring of Christ's Spirit and the birth of the church. But we need to look again at the Pentecost message of unity in the light of our understanding that the confusion of tongues at Babel was God's gift of difference (Gen. 11:1–9). If difference is a gift that helps to prevent domination, surely it is *not* something to be overcome, any more than we would want to overcome God's gift of unity in Christ.

But Peter Gomes has explained, God's goal was further understanding, not abandoning the value of difference. He says:

> The important thing to remember about the Spirit's work at Pentecost, for example, is not the ecstasy which is usually invoked on Pentecost Sunday, the confusion and the excitement and the high energy level. That's an interesting point, but if that were preached in my sermon course I would say that it's a "B" point, not an "A" point. The "A" point is the Spirit-induced understanding. That was the thing that the Spirit did, and that was how the people could say that they each heard in their own language the wonderful works of God. The work of the Spirit is designed to foster understanding and ultimate reconciliation.[12]

God makes unity possible by the gift of the Spirit that enables people of all nations to understand one another, no matter what language is spoken. Acts 2:6 says that "each one heard them speaking in the native language of each." It does not say that people no longer had their own languages and customs but that they could understand one another. This is a very different kind of world from the one envisioned by the builders at Babel, and in it the unity comes, not by building a tower of domination or uniformity, but through communication.

In the book of Acts God's inclusive Spirit makes it possible not only to understand one another in the Spirit, but also for *many voices to be heard* and included at *the center of the discussion. The center has expanded to include those on the margin and the margin is no more.* The structures of domination are challenged as women prophesy, together with men and slaves, and those at the margins of society receive the Spirit:

"In the last days it will be, God declares,
that I will pour out my Spirit upon all flesh,
    and your sons and your daughters shall prophesy,
and your young men shall see visions,
    and your old men shall dream dreams.
Even upon my slaves, both men and women,
    in those days I will pour out my Spirit;
        and they shall prophesy."

                                        (Acts 2:17–18)

The church is born as a community of equals whose unity comes through the love of Christ and is proclaimed and lived out in many and diverse ways (Acts 2:43–47).

God's gift of understanding across difference is expressed in the outpouring of the Spirit which transforms the lives of people and their communities. The Spirit does not so much create the structures and procedures, but rather breaks open structures that confine and separate people so that they can welcome difference and the challenges and opportunities for new understanding that difference brings.[13]

I had a small experience of this breaking down of the barriers of separation on October 7th, 2001, in Washington, D.C., amid a small group of Christian, Jewish, and Muslim women theologians. We had gathered to discuss what we could do as women to promote understanding and peace. Suddenly an announcement came on the news that President Bush was ordering that bombs be dropped on Afghanistan. When the bombs began to fall, one of the Muslim women began to cry. Soon we were all in tears over the misunderstanding and fears being promoted by the media about Islam, and about the use of violence against the people of Afghanistan. In response we agreed to try to create a Sacred Circle study guide that we would distribute on the Web and to work individually to create local groups so that women of different faiths could come together and share sacred Scriptures about peace and pray together for the overcoming of violence in the world. The study guide was never published, but I did follow through and develop an interfaith Sacred Circle group in Guilford, Connecticut, that could study and discuss together. In addition I encouraged my local church to develop a series of adult education forums to better inform congregants about the Muslim faith.

Yet breaking down the barriers and moving toward hospitality can be a tricky process and one fraught with uncertainty. Understanding that the gift of unity is not separate from diversity but is rather an expression of community as people are called to share their many gifts is an important clue to remember. In hospitality we discover, as the writer Audre Lorde has put it, that although there are among us real differences of race, age, gender, and orientation, *these differences are not a problem:* ". . . it is not those differences between us that are separating us. It is rather *our refusal to recognize those differences*, and to examine the distortions which result from our misnaming them and their effects upon human behavior and expectation."[14]

Often we fail to recognize the importance of difference and the ways in which God is glorified through the diversity of persons, cultures, and places in God's created world. We hold on to our prejudices and grudges against people and nations who have wronged us or are "outsiders." We do not even need to begin to speak of Bosnia, Rwanda, or Israel to think of divisions, for in the United States there are persons still unwilling to visit Japan or to speak German because of the Second World War, or afraid to talk with someone wearing a hajib or whose name is Arabic because of September 11. There are also those who would rather think of persons of different sexual orientations from their own as "sexual perverts," and others who consider that if some persons of color have difficulty finding jobs, it's simply because they are lazy.

Yet as followers of Christ who seek to share God's welcome, we are called to recognize difference and respect and honor persons different from ourselves. In this section I invite you to join me in *worrying with God* about the world we live in, and in trying to reimagine the ways God's welcome is at work: in our lives, in our congregations, and in the world around us. Then

we will turn to look at God's practice of hospitality, asking ourselves how we can join in this work of God's welcome.

A DIFFERENT KIND OF UNITY

The stories of Babel and Pentecost show us that God has a different kind of unity in mind. We simply cannot continue to
ignore God's intentions. God does not expect unity that comes
by means of uniformity and the limitation of diversity and difference. Rather, God expects a unity that is rooted in our
recognition that the growing diversity of the church and the
world is a gift of God, rather than a threat to our own comfortable life and faith. In response, we have often tried to live out
unity as unity-in-tension. We need to understand that this
model reinforces dualism and seeks to create unity through
sameness, which does not honor difference.

Unity-in-Tension

One way to move beyond the idea of unity through domination
of the powerful and subordination of the weak, and toward a
welcoming of our neighbor and of difference, is to search for
ways that unity can be held in tension with diversity. This
model of unity and diversity emerged in the ecumenical movement, when churches in the World Council of Churches began
to focus on ways that "all may be one" in Jesus Christ, yet may
manifest that oneness in and through different understandings
of faith and order in confessional families (John 17:21).

But unity-in-tension no longer works well in our extremely
diverse world of many religions, cultures, races, sexual orientations, and nationalities. We can no longer achieve unity by
limiting diversity in the church or in the United Nations.[15]
Diversity now is a major factor in world reality and is, in fact,
frequently one of the key elements of resistance to global
capitalism, American imperialism, and economic, political, and

cultural uniformity. The model of unity in tension is based on structures of domination and on dualistic thinking. It serves those who wish to accumulate power over others and to win unity by setting a norm that denies the dignity and full humanity of others. It is also less likely to serve a desire for unity in Christ in which persons are welcomed and understood in their own language, cultures, and lifestyle. The dualism found in the idea of unity in tension assumes that we can have either *unity or diversity*, and that unity is achieved by limiting or co-opting or destroying difference. Those who don't fit because of their gender, nationality, orientation, or economic situation are considered beyond the limits of diversity.

As we moved toward the end of the twentieth century, it became clear that the global diversity of churches, as well as the diversity within churches in one region, no longer allowed the ecumenical movement to speak only of "ecclesiastical unity" that could be achieved in the churches through common confession of apostolic faith, mutual recognition of baptism, Eucharist and ministry, and through common ways of decision making and teaching authoritatively.[16]

By the time of the Fifth Assembly of the WCC in Nairobi in 1975, the churches had begun to speak of "unity-in-tension" and to recognize the connection of church unity and community to issues of justice and reconciliation.[17] It was still possible to share in the faith that we are made one in Jesus Christ, but no longer possible to imagine that this unity could be established in the churches without new attention to the issues of justice in our world. The churches recognized the changing agenda of the twenty-first century, where unity and diversity is no longer workable as a metaphor for pluralistic communities in which all persons are seeking for a voice and a chance to be heard in their own language of faith.

Let me give you just one small example of the results of this form of thinking. As I mentioned earlier, for more than fifteen years, from the WCC Fifth Assembly in Nairobi in 1975 until 1991, I participated in the WCC Faith and Order Commission discussions of *Baptism, Eucharist and Ministry.*[18] During this time I also served on the Faith and Order Commission of the National Council of Churches. Even though I have been ordained since 1958, the ecumenical discussion still revolved on whether women can fit the traditional male model of Christ's ministry, and why women cause problems in ecumenical cooperation by insisting that their calling to ministry be recognized. Some of the participants seemed to believe that women's ordination pushed the tension too far and destroyed unity.

Instead of trying to hold things together in tension as differences increase, we need to turn to the Scripture to look for other models of unity. As theologian Thomas Best has said, we need to "move beyond unity-in-tension towards a vision of more complete community."[19] One place to look for this vision is Paul's emphasis on the unity of the resurrected body of Christ and the variety of gifts of the Spirit (1 Cor. 12). This new model is a vision from Acts 2:6 or Galatians 3:28 that includes women and men, slave and free, Jew and Greek, Anglo and Arab, gay and straight, young and old, persons with disabilities and abilities, rich and poor, and so much more, as those who speak in the power of the Holy Spirit (Gal. 3:28)

Unity in Hospitality

One possible way of describing this new and different kind of unity is to begin with God's concern to welcome all persons and seek unity through the *practice of hospitality.* Hospitality is an expression of unity without uniformity. Through hospitality community is built out of difference, not sameness; there is no "either/or," "right/wrong," "win/lose." Instead, there are numerous options for ways to faithfully express our unity in Christ and unity among religions and nations. Hospitality in community is a sharing of the openness of Christ to all as he welcomed them into God's kin-dom.[20] Because this unity in Christ has as its purpose the sharing of God's hospitality with the stranger, the one who is "other," it assumes that unity and difference belong together.[21] When they are not together, and unity is achieved through exclusion or domination of those who are different, this is no longer unity in Christ.

The Greek New Testament abounds in exhortations to hospitality. As we noted in chapter 2, New Testament scholar John Koenig describes hospitality as "partnership with strangers" and "the catalyst for creating and sustaining partnerships in the gospel."[22] The Greek word, *philoxenia*, means "love of the stranger." It is the opposite of *xenophobia*, which means "hatred of the stranger" or the one who is different. We are exhorted to hospitality by Paul, who bids us "welcome one another" as Christ has welcomed us (Rom. 15:7). This biblical call for hospitality provides a clue to the idea of welcoming difference, rather than creating an "easy unity" built on compliance to one interpretation of faith in Christ.[23] The example I gave about what happened in the WCC meetings in the 1970s around the validity of women's ordination is an example of easy unity on the basis of excluding women, which does not welcome as Christ would welcome. When we welcome those who come from different contexts and life experiences, we do learn from them, and one of the things we learn is that there are many ways to understand and live out our unity in Christ. These different ways can also open up our churches as we seek to become partners with those who are different by sharing together in mission and service. In this way we leave off building our institutional "towers" and begin to focus on mutual understanding and our calling to serve in the world.

During the WCC Commission on Faith and Order in Santiago de Compostela in 1993, Archbishop Desmond Tutu underlined the importance of such a common agenda for the witness to unity in his reflection on the churches' participation in the struggle against apartheid in South Africa:

> From our experience, then, there can be no question at all that a united church is a far more effective agent for justice and peace against oppression and injustice. It may be that we will find our most meaningful unity as we strive together

for justice and peace. Just imagine what could happen in Northern Ireland and elsewhere if the churches could speak and act as one, for religious differences have exacerbated political, social, and economic differences.[24]

Continuing his interest in working together, Bishop Tutu at the Ninth Assembly of the WCC in Brazil in 2006 marched in the peace vigil against violence and publicly thanked the WCC for its support in the movement to end apartheid and transform South Africa. In a speech during a session on church unity, Tutu expanded the idea of unity from *unity in the church* to *unity in the whole creation*. He spoke on behalf of those whose voices and presence are often not welcome in the churches, saying, "We can only be human together." He singled out God's welcome to gay and lesbian persons and to persons of all faiths as an imperative and said we all belong to one family in which all, *not some*, are *insiders*:

Bush, bin Laden, all belong; gay, lesbian, and so-called straight, all belong and are loved; are precious.[25]

If we spend our time erecting barriers against those who are considered marginal because of their class, race, sexual orientation, or gender, we have moved away from the practice of hospitality. If, on the other hand, we struggle for ways to work through our differences by searching for a common agenda of justice making and transformation, we can move away from practices of unity in tension and toward practices of unity in hospitality.

Unity in hospitality is hard work, and the truth is that it would not be a simple unity to achieve. Here I present four clues from the life and meaning of Christ, which we as Christians are called to emulate. By following these clues we have a better sense of what unity in hospitality might look like.

1. In Christ, unity is a given. As did our foremothers and forefathers, we understand that unity is a gift of God's Spirit, and that our calling is to live out that gift. In Christ, God has made us one and given us the witness of the Holy Spirit to guide and nurture us, so that we might become a community of understanding even in the midst of our alienation. At Pentecost this unity was confirmed by the offer of baptism into Christ and the reception of the Holy Spirit when "about three thousand persons were added" (Acts 2:41).

2. In Christ, difference is a given. God intends for there to be many voices, cultures, and languages and presses the church to be part of every nation and culture, growing and learning from the differences of people in its midst and in the world around it. Dealing with difference in the church does not require limitations but only the willingness to listen and learn together and to find the ways to common service in the name of Christ. One witness of Babel is that diversity is God's gift, which makes possible the riotous diversity of our world.

3. In Christ, hospitality is a given. By his parables of God's kin-dom, Jesus reminds us over and over that God welcomes all those who have been marginal to the established religious and social institutions. Practicing hospitality by seeking justice, peace, and wholeness for all persons and for all creation is a way of living out our faith in Jesus Christ. The pentecostal gift of understanding makes possible hospitality among persons of great diversity as they listen to one another and learn together about the ways of the Spirit in their lives and communities.

4. In Christ, unity is an impossible possibility. Although the church is one in Christ, it lives each day torn by difference while seeking to manifest that oneness. It lives each day with the impossible possibility that one day God will fulfill the unity of the church and mend the creation that has been so torn apart. Then, as I have noted, each of us will cease to live *apart* from one another and become *a part* of God's beautifully diverse creation. At moments when this unity actually occurs among people, it is so surprising that the people are amazed and think, like some of the crowd at Pentecost, that "they are filled with new wine" (Acts 2:13).

A COMMUNITY OF CHRIST

If we accept that a paradigm shift to hospitality can lead to a different kind of unity, then the next question is, how will this shift lead to a different understanding of the church and what would that understanding be? Looked at from the perspective of hospitality, the church becomes "a community of Christ, bought with a price, where everyone is welcome."[26] It is a *community of Christ* because Christ's presence, through the power of the Spirit, constitutes people as a community gathered in Christ's name (Matt. 18:20; 1 Cor. 12:4–6). This community is *bought with a price* because the struggle of Jesus to overcome the structures of sin and death constitutes both the source of new life in the community and its own mandate to continue the same struggle for life on behalf of others (1 Cor. 6:20; Phil. 2:1–11). It is a community *where everyone is welcome* because it gathers around the table of God's hospitality. Its welcome table is a sign of the coming feast of God's mended creation, with the guest list derived from the announcements of the jubilee year and of pentecostal gifts of understanding and inclusion (Luke 14:7–14; Acts 2:1–21).

The Source of Unity

In this understanding of church as a community of Christ where everyone is welcome, the *source of unity* is the gift of Christ's presence in our midst, calling us to be open to others. The *test of that unity* is how well our churches break down barriers and welcome those who have been at the margins of church and society (Luke 4: 18–19). One way the church has been tested in its hospitality over the last forty years has been in the push for full inclusion and partnership in the life of the church by women of all colors. In many denominations women are now able to participate fully as pastors, elders, and deacons. Yet even in these churches they often find themselves limited and marginalized in decision making.

The struggles of women for full inclusion in the life of the churches is documented in the reports of the Ecumenical Decade of Churches in Solidarity with Women and the Community of Women and Men in the Church study that preceded it. As Musimbi Kanyoro said in her sermon at the festival mentioned earlier in Harare, which preceded the Eighth Assembly of the WCC:

> We can no longer just call for solidarity. We need to be part of a redefining and redesigning process for all the changes we hope for this decade. . . . We will not accept our gifts being minimized, but rather we will lift up all the gifts of the people of God.[27]

For a decade, the women and men in the churches of the WCC had been considering how the church might act in solidarity with women, along with men. Five years into the Decade, a series of "Living Letters" were sent to the churches, letters written by women in churches throughout the world in response to Jesus' question, "Woman, why are you weeping?" Five years later, at the end of the Decade, again a letter was written to representatives from the WCC churches gathered at the Eighth Assembly in Harare, Zimbabwe. The letter stated:

> We hold firmly to the vision of a human community where the participation of each and every one is valued, where no one is excluded on the basis of race, sex, age, religion or cultural practice, where diversity is celebrated as God's gift to the world.
>
> To this end, we call upon you to initiate actions to correct the gender imbalances that exist in your midst, and make all levels of administration in churches and ecumenical organizations accessible and just for women. We urge you to encourage more women to take up leadership roles and support them so that they can offer new understandings of and ways of using power.[28]

If we spend our time erecting barriers against those who are considered marginal because of class, race, sexual orientation or gender, we have moved away from the paradigm of hospitality. If, on the other hand, we struggle for ways to work through our differences without demeaning those we consider unimportant, we can move beyond unity and diversity and toward unity in hospitality as a church and in society.

Liberating Difference

We have been talking a great deal about difference thus far. As I have noted elsewhere, *difference* is a very important topic to our understanding of hospitality for two reasons. First, it is important because the postcolonial world we live in is a world of hybrid societies and people who are in search of their own identity and of ways to be neighbor to one another across barriers of race, nationality, language, gender, class, sexual orientation, abilities, and so much more. It is also important because difference is used as a category of exclusion in patriarchal thinking and social political structures.

By focusing on the problems of difference, we can search for ways to gather as *communities* of faith committed to sharing in God's welcome of the stranger and committed to the practice of *hospitality*. With that in mind, and just as a way of further reflection, I would like you to think about how to turn essentializing and destructive difference into a form of liberating, or what Iris Marion Young calls *emancipatory* difference.

As we have seen, one way to confront destructive forms of difference is to understand how difference itself has become a category of exclusion and domination in our postcolonial world. Unless we confront the misuse of difference, there is no integrity in our talk about a God who welcomes all people, or in our actions as participants in that welcome. God is an *inside out God*, who created a world of riotous difference in which creation and creature alike show forth a rainbow variety of God's goodness. God's intention would seem to be, not to eliminate difference, but to make it possible to communicate across differences of language, culture, and social location (Gen. 11:1–9; Acts 2:1–12).[29]

Understanding difference as a gift of God may help us search for ways that difference may become liberating or emancipatory in our lives. Drawing in part on the work of Iris Marion Young in *Justice and the Politics of Difference*, I want to develop three ways that provide us with clues as to how we can reclaim difference as an important aspect of our work together as postcolonial subjects.[30]

The first clue on the way to claiming emancipatory difference is to *stop essentializing difference*. The essentializing of difference makes it possible to use differences as a structural weapon of oppression. Essentialists argue that differences of race, sex, class, and sexual orientation are *part of created nature and cannot be changed*. From this perspective, it becomes possible to justify oppression, poverty, exploitation and imperialism by declaring that the dominating group has been created to, for instance, "rule the world." For example, the story that women were created first, and fell second, is used to reinforce the idea that they are by nature inferior, dependent on men, and sources of sin and corruption. Today, we see this idea reinforced so that if all women need to belong to a man and to bear children, then a childless African woman loses her identity, and a lesbian woman is unnatural or an abomination. When we stop essentializing difference, we must reject stereotypes and disentangle culturally created ideas from claims of naturalness.

The second clue to claiming emancipatory difference is the importance of *building relational difference*. As Iris Young has written: "Difference emerges not as a description of the attributes of a group, but as a function of the relations between groups and the interaction of groups with institutions."[31] Recognizing the overlapping qualities of social groupings allows a group to be both different and the same. This recognition provides the freedom for a particular social group to define itself, and yet recognize its interdependent relationships *within the group*. Differences within groups can then be honored. At that point there is *no longer a need for essentializing difference* or enforcing conformity.

A third clue on our journey toward emancipatory difference is the importance of building on relational difference by *forming coalitions across difference*. This work requires the development of networks that can sustain groups in their struggles and provide opportunities for partnership as postcolonial subjects. The work of justice and the mending of creation is not limited to one continent or group. In each social location there are people willing "to put their bodies on the line" with others as they join a God who is inside out (Rom. 12:1–2). Certainly the creation of the alliance between the Circle of Concerned African Women Theologians and two divisions of Yale University, the Divinity School and the Department of Epidemiology and Public Health of Yale Medical School, illustrates that coalitions of difference can prosper and effect change despite major differences. The Circle, as mentioned earlier, is a group of women from Christian, Muslim, Jewish, and African Independent Church traditions and represents women from African, Indian, and European heritage. The women of Yale Divinity School represented several racial and ethnic groups as well as different faith traditions. The group from the Center for Interdisciplinary Research on AIDS (CIRA) at the Yale School of Public Health was also racially and religiously diverse. Our partnership to create HIV/AIDS projects that would help religious communities in Africa respond to the AIDS pandemic continued for five years and included twelve women from the Circle who studied at the Divinity School and at CIRA. When the U.S. government canceled the funding, the connections among the Circle and the women who had designed projects and the two Yale groups continued. In fact, an additional coalition, for Roman Catholic women in Africa, was started by Margaret Farley, a Sister of Mercy at Yale, when she saw the importance of the Circle for the women of Africa. This new group, called the All Africa Conference: Sister to Sister, is a coalition involving women in many African countries along

with women religious in the United States. These projects illustrate that such coalitions are possible, if improbable! Notes
Margaret Farley,

> Out of the experience of such partnerships come impera-
> tives for all—imperatives to care for one another and, in
> doing so, to resist the forces of diminishment and death. It
> is possible to share journeys, both marvelous and terrible,
> from which none of us can turn back.[32]

As strangers to ourselves and to so many other people, we
have this possibility of learning to trust ourselves and others
whom we encounter as we share in God's concern for us all and
for all creation. We are challenged to recognize the religious
and cultural pluralism of our societies and search for ways of
living together in the midst of difference. As Diana Eck has
said about her Pluralism Project at Harvard,

> Whether in India or America, whether in [New Hampshire]
> or at Harvard University, the challenge for all of us today is
> how to shape societies, nations, neighborhoods, and univer-
> sities that now replicate and potentially may reconfigure the
> differences that have long divided humankind.[33]

Hospitality is not *the only* answer to difference, but it is one
way to respond to this challenge. It points us to the future that
God intends, where riotous difference is welcomed! Hospitality will not *make us safe*, but it will lead us to risk joining in the
work of mending the creation without requiring those whom
we encounter to become like us.

Questions for Thought

1. What towers of difference do you see being built or still
   standing tall in today's world?
2. Are you familiar with instances of your faith community
   working to hear the stories of other voices? What con-

crete examples can you give of how that happens? What might those stories teach you about your own community's "ability to hear" like those at Pentecost?

3. How do you deal with difference in group situations? How do you feel when you behave this way? How do those around you respond?

4. Give an example of how you might seek unity through hospitality in your ministry.

4

Reframing a Theology of Hospitality

We turn now to *reframing the idea of hospitality through identifying characteristics of God's gift of welcome.* Some would say our grammar and vocabulary help the way we view or "frame" our world. If, for example, we have a large vocabulary with which to describe bird characteristics, we have an easier time identifying a particular bird. Similarly, those sailors of the South Pacific who used "stick maps" to sail and paddle from island to unseen island could precisely describe the waves and currents and thus travel great distances by "reading" the ocean. My own love of and success at sailing grew from an early "framing" of the vocabulary of the wind and tides of Long Island Sound imparted to me by my mother, who spent many hours teaching me to sail when I was a youngster.

"Reframing," according to George Lakoff, means changing the way we see the world and therefore the way we speak and act in the world.[1] Let me give an example. A recent tragedy in Connecticut has reframed the way the public views certain house robberies. A woman and her two daughters were senselessly murdered during the burglary of their home by two men. Since that event, such crimes are now labeled "home invasions" and numerous calls for stricter legislation have surfaced. The public consciousness of household burglaries has now been upgraded or reframed to conjure the gruesome images created and evoked by the new phrase "home invasion."

In light of Lakoff's idea of reframing, in this chapter I look at the frames of hospitality, that is, the ways we have traditionally imagined hospitality that limit its effectiveness as a response to the fear of difference in a pluralistic and dangerous world. As in earlier chapters, I use biblical stories to explore what God intends for our understanding of difference and what these interpretations tell us about hospitality. The Bible can be a source of guidance on both hospitality and inhospitality.

FRAMING AND REFRAMING

The theme of the Ninth Assembly of the World Council of Churches meeting in Porto Alegre, Brazil, in 2006, was transformation. The 600 delegates from 340 churches around the world met to worship and study together, hear reports, plan for the coming seven years, and elect a continuing Central Committee, which would oversee the work of the WCC until the next assembly seven years hence. Along with the delegates, advisers, resource people, and staff, another 2,000 people gathered to share the events and create their own workshops around the theme *God in Your Grace Transform the World!*

Every day around 8:00 a.m. we climbed aboard buses and went to the Pontifical University, the site of the meeting. We began each day with worship and Bible study and ended it with prayers and an 8:00 p.m. ride back to our various hotels for dinner.

The subject of each day's plenaries was transformation, but there were also meetings and workshops on issues such as persons with disabilities, human sexuality, religious pluralism, and the scandal of poverty; a special youth assembly; and two marches against violence, one sponsored by the WCC's project on Overcoming Violence Against Women, and the second a walk for peace in the world, led by two Nobel Prize recipients, Bishop Desmond Tutu, and Adolfo Pérez Esquivel. I was there as a resource person for the study process called "Women's Voices and Visions on Being Church," which had been initiated in 1998 at the end of the Ecumenical Decade of the Churches in Solidarity with Women. We had met in Asia in 2000, Latin America in 2001, Africa in 2003, and in North America in 2004. Eleni Kasselouri-Hatzivassiliadi from Greece and a member of the Greek Orthodox Church, was a member of the international steering group. She summed up the process at our final session in New York, saying, "I didn't know what to expect, but I have felt welcomed. I have not only learned about the other, but more about myself and my own tradition as well. Now I need to go home and work on seeing my own faith from a new perspective."[2]

The role of our international steering committee was to stress the need to hear women's calls for change in the church and continue to press member churches to fully include women in all the orders of church life. The most important part of the Assembly for me was the opportunity to see so many of my friends from around the globe, to make new friends, and to build ever stronger women's advocacy networks.

In the midst of programs about unity, peace, water, refugees, violence against women, U.S. imperialism, HIV/AIDS, and much more, the practice of hospitality was literally being reframed, as strangers joined together in their work to transform the world, beginning with themselves and the churches of which they were a part. One issue of the newspaper *Transforma Mundo* focused on the theme of true hospitality, showing that here hospitality was being reimagined, as were many other aspects of the Christian faith.[3] The conditions and events leading to this reframing included the effects of plurality on people's daily lives, which made it necessary for them to find new and untried ways of relating to and understanding people from different religious traditions. Increasing religious extremism has also hastened the need for interfaith dialogue. And last, religion is playing an ever-greater role in both ethnic and international conflicts, so that political conversations that never considered faith and religion now must take those traditions into account, thus broadening the frames for negotiation and conflict resolution.

Making a Change

While the idea of hospitality *sounds good*, it is difficult to practice. People often happily embrace the concept when they imagine it means having friends over for dinner or serving coffee and goodies after church. But hospitality with strangers evokes a very different feeling. I wrote about the difficulties in my book *Church in the Round*[4] where I conclude, "Hospitality is an expression of unity without uniformity, because unity in Christ has as its purpose the sharing of God's hospitality with the stranger, the one who is 'other.'"[5] I also described there the "deformation" of the idea of God's special welcome to the Hebrew people (see also chapter 2). By the word "deformation" I mean literally deforming or taking apart and reshaping a previous understanding. No matter how we attempt to challenge difference and the use of strangeness or "otherness" to exclude, ignore, or dominate those who are different, we still find ourselves *constrained by difference*. The solution is to reframe the way we practice hospitality and thus deform, re-form, or reshape our previous notions.

This kind of reframing is important for several reasons. First, it is necessary because hospitality is often associated with such things as "terminal niceness" like tea parties and the work of women in their homes, or even as the vocation of prostitutes in the street. Second, we usually limit our hospitality or welcome to those who are like us in terms of class, race, nationality, language, economic position—unlike the idea of "unity without uniformity," which requires different actions. Third, hospitality is also subject to deformation when it is practiced as a way of caring for so called "inferior people" by those who are more advantaged and able to prove their superiority by being "generous," rather than using a model of partnership. We need to end the "lady bountiful" frame and strive to meet others as they are, not as objects of our charity, but persons in their own right, capable of making choices about their destiny. If we insist they dress as we do and follow the same manners, we are not exercising hospitality but "reforming" others to match our expectations. In a recent conference on Muslim-Christian dialogue, a Jewish participant said, "We tend to want to see the others through our own eyes. The path to understanding is to see others the way they see themselves, not the way we want to see them."[6]

Steps to Reframing

In order to successfully reframe our idea of hospitality, we must, ethicist Rebecca Todd Peters argues, do two things: first, acknowledge the inhospitality of our ancestors toward indigenous peoples, and second, challenge the idea that the Great Commission in Matthew 28:18–20 means that we should go out and create a global Christian empire.[7]

> And Jesus came and said to them, "All authority in heaven and on earth has been given to me. Go therefore and make disciples of all nations, baptizing them in the name of the Father and of the Son and of the Holy Spirit, and teaching them to obey everything that I have commanded you. And remember, I am with you always, to the end of the age."

These words from Matthew about going to teach, preach, and baptize in Jesus' name echo the imperial Roman practice of expansion to "the ends of the earth" and have been used by colonial empires ever since to justify colonization, domination, and forced conversion to Christianity.[8] Peters argues that before we can move away from such stereotypical attitudes about hospitality, we have to decolonize our minds. Doing so entails no longer isolating ourselves from a diversity of people and experiences, recognizing the signs and effects of white power and privilege, and noticing and doing something about the fact that the United States uses an inordinate amount of the world's resources for its population. Peters warns that if we do not change, "our heritage and identity as people of faith is tragically misshapen, distorted, and destructive of our own souls as people of faith created to live in justice-seeking community with the rest of God's good creation."[9]

Peters points to the false practice of hospitality as global mission as an example of the kind of hospitality we must move away from. Churches that understand Christianity as "universal truth" and assume a dualistic worldview in which the "others" are inferior to us in every way, also believe *those people* need to be saved, dominated, and controlled by people in the churches of the former colonizing nations. Decolonizing the Christian worldview, she notes, requires that we reach out in partnership to the strangers around us. To do this, we must reject the imperial idea that there exists one dominant truth, and try and divest ourselves of the cultural sin of self-superiority and domination of others. This decolonizing allows us to begin to listen to those we consider "other." And once we begin to listen, we may discover that our assumptions are in error, which may in turn lead to new understandings that our previous frames prevented us from seeing or even imagining.

Rather than focusing only on ourselves and our own individual actions, we must also look at hospitality in terms of social structures of justice and of partnership across barriers of difference. When we decolonize our minds, we begin thinking from the margins rather than from the center. We *reframe hospitality as a form of partnership with the ones we call "other,"* rather than as a form of charity or entertainment. One way to go about this *metanoia,* or conversion in our thinking, is to reexamine the biblical tradition in order better to understand what God's welcome and hospitality are all about. In the Bible, God's welcome—hospitality—has at least four overlapping central components: (1) unexpected divine presence; (2) advocacy for the marginalized; (3) mutual welcome; and (4) creation of community.

Unexpected divine presence has its classical expression in the story of Abraham and Sarah at the oaks of Mamre, who entertain, without knowing it, God's messengers (Gen. 18:1–15). In the New Testament, Hebrews 13:2 reminds us of this story, saying, "some have entertained angels unawares" (KJV). The Emmaus text in Luke 24:13–35 contains similar themes, with the discovery of the risen Christ interpreting Scripture and the breaking of bread. Matthew 25:31–46, sometimes called the judgment of the nations, can sound very judgmental to us, but one way of interpreting this text is that Jesus is telling his own story so that his disciples will know where to find him. That is, when we show hospitality to those in prison and those who are sick, hungry, thirsty, and naked, we discover the risen Christ, who has chosen to be there with those who need God's help and ours. By this reading, the text is not so much an agenda of dos and don'ts but a promise that Christ will be there, as unexpectedly as it may seem to us, among broken people, as well as in the breaking of bread. Our biblical traditions remind us that, in the practice of hospitality, we entertain Christ unawares and are surprised by the unexpected divine presence.

In both the Hebrew Bible and the New Testament, God's hospitality also involves *welcome of and advocacy for the marginalized*. In the Hebrew Scriptures the people were exhorted not to oppress the stranger, because they were once strangers in Egypt (Exod. 23:9). We are called to recognize the marginalized and treat them with equal dignity. Because of God's welcome and deliverance, we are to welcome others, as in the Christmas enactment of "no room at the inn," called Las Posadas.[10] In Las Posadas, the community reenacts Mary and Joseph's journey as they travel through the village knocking on doors asking for a place to stay. It is the innkeeper who shares his only space with the strangers. This reenactment reminds the community to open their doors to the stranger and share what they have.

Mutual welcome is another characteristic of hospitality. Hospitality is a particular theme in Paul's letters as the apostle seeks to create community in his little house churches. Whether within the community or between the community and those outside, the hospitality he speaks of is to be one of mutual welcome. He

urges members to live in harmony with one another, in particular, overcoming the disagreements between Gentile and Jewish
Christians over the requirements of the Jewish law. At the beginning of his letter to the Romans, in Romans 1:11–12, Paul speaks
of longing that he and those in Rome may be "mutually encouraged by each other's faith." At the end of the letter, in Romans
15:7, Paul concludes two chapters about disputes over eating
together with what John Koenig calls the climax of his argument:
"Welcome one another, therefore, just as Christ has welcomed
you, for the glory of God."

For Paul, Koenig believes, "everyday welcomings of the
'other,' especially at table, are really acts of worship 'for the
glory of God.'"[11] The words we use to describe hospitality in
the Scriptures themselves illustrate this. Both *philoxenia* and
Latin *hostes* imply a reciprocal relationship of give-and-take,
meaning host and guest sometimes exchange roles. Koenig calls
hospitality "delight in the guest-host relationship."[12]

This insight hints at the fourth characteristic of God's welcome: hospitality involves the *creation of community*. Jesus is
often at table, eating, in the Gospels. And Paul picks this up
and makes table sharing a key to building up a partnership, or
koinonia, among the hybrid church communities, whose members come from different classes, religious backgrounds, genders, races, and ethnic groups.

Koinonia, community in partnership, was understood as
cooperation around a divine project, around a commitment to
live out the lifestyle of Jesus Christ.[13] I often describe this partnership as a new focus of relationship in Jesus Christ that sets
us free for others and is nurtured through continuing commitment and common struggle in a wider community context. In
order to nurture congregations in cooperation and trust in God
and one another, Paul urges the practice of hospitality. Koenig
describes the role of hospitality in creating community: "We
might call *hospitality the catalyst for creating and sustaining partnerships in the gospel.* Within these partnerships all members,
even God as director, will play the role of stranger."[14]

GOD'S HOSPITALITY: REFRAMING SAFETY IN BIBLICAL TRADITION

Because some people might be fearful of partnering with ones on the margin, I want to discuss how we can understand "safety" in the Scriptures as we further explore hospitality as it relates to God's welcome in the biblical narrative. On September 11, 2001, we discovered that even North America is not immune from danger, and especially since then, in the United States the search for safe space has been a primary focus for people in regard to where they live, travel, work, go to school, and gather together, in both large and small groups. We have long known that, for many people, the world has not been a *safe space* for quite a while, but now suddenly we are all confronted with the fragility of peace and safety and the desire to ensure our own safety.

In addition to seeking physical safety, many people seek safety and calm in prayer and communal worship, or turn to Scripture for words of comfort and the assurance that nothing can separate us from God's love (Rom. 8:39). Yet, like the world around us, Scripture itself is often *dangerous to our health*. Reading the Bible through the lens of our culture, presuppositions, language, and religious traditions—and we all do—affects the message we hear. Sometimes that message is not safe for the person hearing it: battered women hear that they should be loyal to their husbands, even if it might kill them. Non-Christians hear that they will be condemned to hell, and even if they do not read the text themselves, some Christians are more than happy to quote such passages to them. Lesbian, bisexual, gay, and transgender persons find that they are targets for discrimination and violence. You can make your own list of the dangers!

I invite you to consider the particular problem of safety when offering hospitality, knowing that it is directly tied to our concerns for all manner of safety in the world in which we live and where many suffer and die unnecessarily. Our search will be in an improbable place: the book of Ruth, an irenic story

about hospitality with a "happy ending." Old Testament
scholar Katharine Sakenfeld, in her commentary on Ruth even
presents it as an eschatological image of God's shalom celebrated in human community.[15] Yet as we will see, hidden in the
story are many dangers. But before we turn to Ruth, we must
explore three topics: the meaning of safe space; searching Scriptures for that space; and developing a spirituality of listening
that is not harmful to ourselves and our neighbors, be they near
or far.

The Meaning of Safe Space

We all know in our hearts what *safe space* means, and we could
give many descriptions of what it could mean. These descriptions
include safety from violence and attack like that on September
11, but they stretch further to family, food and shelter, and well-
being—the basics of hospitality. We begin our search for such a
safe space by looking at the biblical understanding of safety.

Long before the uprooting of people through war, violence,
and economic displacement produced the refugee problems of
our own time, the Hebrew and Christian traditions acknowl-
edged the need for sanctuary and the protection of the one
seeking a refuge or home. Ever since Adam and Eve, the first
refugees, people have been searching for safe places in which to
dwell, and as New Testament scholar John Elliott has said,
"The Bible is an inspired and inspiring record of displaced and
dispossessed peoples who have found a communal identity and
home with God."[16]

The Hebrew concept of sanctuary is rooted in the tradition
of the *cities of refuge* (Exod. 21:13; Num. 35:9–11). These
"cities" were holy or sanctified places, often a temple, where
God and the people of Israel protected those who sought
refuge. Deuteronomy 19:7–10 says in part: "Therefore I com-
mand you: You shall set apart three cities . . . so that the blood
of an innocent person may not be shed in the land that the
LORD your God is giving you as an inheritance." This provision
was usually intended to protect those who were guilty of invol-

untary murder and extended not only to the Israelites, but also to any "resident or transient alien among them" (Num. 35:15). The theme of God's provision of refuge and safety for an exile people runs through the Hebrew Scriptures, and in Ruth, as in Numbers 35:15, includes the more expansive idea that such refuge extends to all persons, and not just the Hebrew people.

The word "sanctuary" comes from the Latin *sanctus*, which means "holy." The Latin *sanctus* comes from the Hebrew *kaddish*, meaning "holy." The right of protection for all persons is derived from God's holiness and provides the basic theological understanding of hospitality in both Hebrew and Christian Scriptures: Human beings are created by God and are to be holy, and to be treated as holy or sacred: "You shall be holy, for I the LORD your God am holy" says Leviticus 19:2. Elie Wiesel reminds us, in his article "The Refugee," that sanctuary or sacred space refers not just to buildings, but also to human beings:

> Every human being is a dwelling of God—man or woman or child, Christian or Jewish or Buddhist [or Muslim]. Any person, by virtue of being a son or a daughter of humanity, is a living sanctuary whom nobody has the right to invade.[17]

Wiesel's is an important reminder that it is not just buildings, or national security, but *human lives* that are sacred.

Every person as a dwelling of God is an important part of the New Testament message as well. In the Gospels Jesus teaches us what it means to care for our neighbor in the parable of the Good Samaritan (Luke 10:30–37) and to welcome all persons, particularly those who are most marginal, to our table (Luke 14:12–14). In Matthew 25:31–45 Jesus even tells us that he is present to us when we share in his hospitality to those who are sick, hungry, and in prison.

This theme continues in Paul's images of God's welcome and safety and Paul's urging us to "welcome one another, therefore, just as Christ has welcomed you, for the glory of God" (Rom. 15:7). In Romans 8:39 Paul makes clear that the worst that can happen to us will still not separate us from God in Jesus Christ. The writer of Revelation ends with the assurances that God will "wipe away every tear" and "death will be no more" in the "new heaven and new earth" (Rev. 21:1–4). Thus a basic biblical theme and message is played out around the human search for safety and well-being as an opportunity to offer hospitality as God's welcome. As Walter Brueggemann has put it:

> The Bible is forceful and consistent in its main theological theme. That claim concerns the conviction that the God who creates the world in love redeems the world in suffering and will consummate the world in joyous well-being.[18]

Searching the Scriptures for Safe Space

Given Scripture's concern for the safety and well-being of the creation and all its creatures through mandates of hospitality, why is it that Scripture itself can be so dangerous in its message and so contradictory to God's offer of safety and welcome for all? The answer is rather obvious: Both its writing and its interpretation happen in a flawed world, in which persons celebrate a faith in God's presence among them that is incarnated in the biases of their particular culture, language, and religious tradition. Resolving this threat requires *eternal vigilance!* Used in the wrong way, the Bible is often like *The Monster Book of Monsters* that Harry Potter got as a present from Hagrid in *The Prisoner of Azkaban*. To keep it from snapping and smashing his fingers, Harry had to capture it and secure it with a belt. The big beautiful green leather book lettered in gold turned out to be a danger unless you could learn the secret of safe handling![19]

Like Harry, we have to know how to approach the Bible so that we are not taken unaware, as he was. Many of us were taught about the Bible in church school or college or in Bible study groups at church, yet biblical illiteracy is quite common, even among those who attended church school. Tom Grant, a longtime sixth-grade teacher at my local church, often talks about the paucity of biblical knowledge among his students. What can we do to ensure that we are reading the Bible with as much clarity as possible and that the Bible can, in turn, read us so we can accurately recognize God's hospitality? We can begin by bearing in mind at least four cautions as we read the texts: reading with a hermeneutic of suspicion, recognizing and confronting patriarchy, looking for the contradictions, and, finally, reading with a hermeneutic of commitment.

1. Reading with a hermeneutic of suspicion. Even if we do not imitate Harry by hiding the Bible under the floorboards, we do need to approach the text with what scholars call a *hermeneutic of suspicion*. That is, we must pay attention to the hidden messages in the Bible's writing and interpretation, all the while celebrating the insights we receive from the texts as they are inspired in our lives by the Holy Spirit. For many of us, the dilemma looks a lot like this description from Mary Ann Tolbert:

> For Protestants, the Bible is not simply a source of *knowledge* about God or the early Christians or the Hebrew people; it is, rather, a source for *experiencing, hearing,* God or God-in-Jesus in each present moment of life. Nevertheless . . . the Bible continues to exercise over women, and other oppressed groups like homosexuals, a form of "textual harassment."[20]

"Textual harassment" describes situations in which a particular Bible text is used to limit or harm someone. Particular interpretations of Scripture have been used to force women, people of racial/ethnic groups, and LGBT persons to adopt specific behaviors and restrict them from others. The Bible has been used as justification for racism, sexism, heterosexism, ableism, and colonialism, as we discussed in chapter 2. For example, for centuries women were told to cover their heads and to keep silent in the churches because of their inferior status—created second, sinned first. The Orthodox tradition continues to require head coverings for women, and a number of denominations refuse to permit women to be ordained. Scripture has also been used against gays and lesbians, who have been refused access to ordination or membership in many faith traditions unless they denounced their homosexuality.

2. Recognizing and confronting patriarchy. Dealing with textual harassment begins with *confronting patriarchy* or what Elisabeth Schüssler Fiorenza calls *kyriarchy* (rule of the lord) as we discover it in our own lives and in the cultural world of the Bible, the Bible itself, and interpretations of the Bible.[21] In this task we are greatly helped by feminist writers and interpreters in recognizing that biblical texts are historical and conditioned, and require careful and critical analysis of their context and development. Feminist interpreters are not alone by any means in this insight, but they pay particular attention to the way the biblical literature was shaped by a patriarchal culture, worldview, and interpretation.

In seeking *the full humanity of all women, together with all men*, Christian and Jewish feminist interpreters of all colors and nationalities understand that their quest is for a way of participating with God in the concern for restoring human wholeness and relationship, and for the mending of creation. This is no small task, because the Bible has been a source of dangerous justification for racism, sexism, heterosexism, ableism, colonialism, ecological destruction, and on and on. At the same time, it is also a source of safety and hope for a New Creation. Mary Ann Tolbert describes our hermeneutical or interpretive dilemma as a "struggle against God as enemy assisted by God as helper, or one must defeat the Bible as patriarchal authority by using the Bible as liberator."[22]

3. Looking for the contradictions. A hermeneutic of suspicion involves looking beneath the surface of the text for the contradictions between what the text is telling us and what is actually happening in the events and in the teachings of the culture. Stories carry a variety of meanings that may set up contradictions explicitly within the story. At other times, the contradiction may stem from our cultural associations with the story. I describe this further using the example of Ruth and Naomi. However, we must acknowledge these contradictions, as difficult, confusing, or dangerous as they may seem.

4. Reading with a hermeneutic of commitment. How can we search for safe space in Scripture when such harmful messages can be taken from the biblical text? A hermeneutic of suspicion is important, but it is not enough. Those who want to wrestle with Scripture and its many meanings are still trying to hear the message of God's news through all the text's ambiguities and contradictions. To do this, we must also approach the text with a *hermeneutic of commitment.* This commitment means believing that God might provide a safe space in the text that speaks to us in some way, if only by telling us that this is a text in which the message is *thou shalt not!* do what it describes.

REFRAMING A TEXT: RUTH'S STORY

In our search for safe space and God's welcome, I want to use the familiar hospitality story of Ruth and Naomi. Here we have a little book in the Bible that teaches us about opposition to racism, loyalty to one another, and God's fulfillment of our longing for safety in community. Yet the same story carries other, potentially dangerous messages about such things as marriage customs, the value of male heirs, sexual favors, the power of rich males, the obligation of young women to their mothers-in-law, and the love of two women consummated in heterosexual marriage. In some communities, the levirate marriage custom in which the nearest male relative of the deceased husband is assigned to marry the widow still survives. In the book of Ruth, Naomi recognizes and proclaims to her daughters-in-law the futility of producing new sons for them to marry. She then encourages the young women to return to their own homes.

Ruth, however, refuses to return to her home and accompanies Naomi to Bethlehem. This establishes two possibly harmful cultural precedents. The first occurs when Naomi directs Ruth to present herself to Boaz, a cousin of Naomi's husband, following the traditional custom. Today we still see women reinforcing that a woman needs a man to survive. A friend in Kenya once told me that when her brother-in-law died, suddenly his family came to her sister's home and tried to take all the contents. They then announced that her dead husband's brother would now marry her sister. Her sister was a respected physician, and while she had never expected that such a thing would happen, she also had a difficult time refusing the family's demands.

Second, in some Asian cultures, the allegiance of Ruth to Naomi creates a different, yet equally harmful precedent. Mothers-in-law can expect total submission from their daughters-in-law. In some instances, male grandchildren must even be sent to their paternal grandparents when they are five.

Nonetheless, the story of Ruth continues to signify the love of one person for another. In this case, the two happen both to be women. Whether or not the love conveyed was a sexual one we do not know. What we do know is that the situation of two widowed women required remedying. Although Ruth was allowed to glean in the fields to collect food to share with Naomi, Naomi realized the importance and power of a rich male, particularly if the male was a relative. And she also knew that an heir—again, especially a male heir—was to be sought. She then encourages Ruth to place herself in a compromising situation so that Boaz can "do the right thing." Although Naomi was probably not thinking of the line of succession to David, the writers were aware of this eventuality.

Attending to Context

Even with a book as irenic as Ruth we are constantly caught in the struggle to use a hermeneutic of suspicion while still allowing the text the safety to speak its own word. Sakenfeld recognizes this and urges us to read Ruth as *one story* of the true meaning of human community "rather than as a prescription for how that community ought always to be organized."[23] If we don't follow her advice, the "common" frame of the text becomes harmful to women's health—for example, in its cultural assumptions that marriage is the solution to economic insecurity—and might possibly support levirate marriage today or Ruth's total obedience to her mother-in-law's suggestions regarding Boaz.

These dangers are clearly no more serious than those facing women today, as Sakenfeld has also written about in her book *Just Wives?* where she tells the true story of a young girl in the Philippines who, like so many others, was recruited as a "dancer" overseas to help support her family. She ignored her pastor's warnings that she would probably be forced into sexual slavery or prostitution, saying, "Ruth put herself forward attractively to a rich man in hopes that he would marry her and take care of her family. I am doing the same. I hope a rich man from that country will choose me to marry and will look after me and my family. God made things turn out right for Ruth and God will take care of me too."[24]

Two important clues to reframing a difficult text in our search for God's counsel are (1) attention to standpoint dependence and (2) attention to context. Let us look first at standpoint dependence. We all know that "what we see depends on where we are standing," yet we often disregard this truism when we look at a biblical text. We must always begin by paying attention to our own bias—which comes from our class, race, sexual orientation, religious affiliation, age, ability, and so on. The book of Ruth looks one way to a Christian woman in Taiwan who grieves that she must, as soon as her only son turns five, give him up to her mother-in-law to raise. It looks another way to an interracial couple who value the courage of the Moabite woman Ruth and her Israelite husbands—first Naomi's son Mahlon, and then Naomi's relative Boaz in Judah—who did not let their ethnic and religious differences keep them apart. Our social location and religious traditions affect the way we see the text, and we need to be aware of that if we are committed to hearing the text beyond our own biases. The same kind of bias was at work in the writing and editing of the text as well as in its various interpretations. Therefore, asking the question of where we, the texts, and its interpreters are "coming from" is part of our searching process.

However, it is not enough just to read a story or to read interpretations of a story. Context is equally important. We must seek help in order to know how the text was compiled, its position in the Judeo-Christian tradition, and the context out of which it comes. This is why writers of commentaries spend a great deal of time in their introductions providing information about the dates, geographic and cultural location, writers, and intentions and themes of a Scripture text.[25] At the same time, understanding the context of the text in the wider Scripture is important, so that we are able to recognize changes, contrasts, and confirmations in the text by looking at parallel or similar texts and at the way the text is retold if it appears in another or later book of the Bible. And most certainly the context of those interpreting the text and listening to the text affects what is heard and said. For instance, the description in Ruth about a safe world where customs can protect widows, 4:7–12, is particularly jarring and out of place to us in this world of tension and fighting in the Middle East and elsewhere and where people far and near face chaos and destruction of life and property. The context of our present search is that right now *nothing in our lives feels very safe!*

Using both a hermeneutic of suspicion and contextual interpretation enables us to hear the Scriptures in a new way. We begin by trying to discern God's welcome. But often, as we dispute the texts and the interpretations we have been told or read, we begin to value our own way of thinking more than the texts and, rather than listening to the texts, we begin to do *all the talking!* In so doing, *we ourselves become dangerous to the Scriptures*, because we deny them the safe space to be read, digested, and heard. So, along with a hermeneutic of suspicion and commitment, we need a hermeneutic of silence and listening that will enable us to hear the word for our day.

Developing a Spirituality of Listening

As we read and interpret the Bible, we need a lot of silence, so as not to place our own frames on the story. Barbara Lundblad said in her 2000 Beecher Lectures at Yale Divinity School, there should be pauses when we read the Bible, pauses in which "conversation could go on in our hearts about what is said and not said."[26] In these pauses we provide *a safe space for the Scriptures to speak* a new word to us. The open space or silence may be able to draw us into the text so that we can hear anew what it is saying to us. In this open space, by attending to the text itself and to the text of the community of interpretation, we may find a meeting place between the two where something happens and "God brings forth a new word."[27] In this hermeneutical space of listening and responding with our hearts, we may discover new clues about our insights into the text.

This is certainly what happened to Katharine Sakenfeld as she considered the ending of Ruth.[28] In listening over and over both to the text and to the meanings given to it by women in different communities around the world and then pondering them in her heart, she discovered that the various interpretations came out of both the context of women's lives and the context of the story. This realization became for Sakenfeld a clue to understanding the story's "happy ending" as Ruth and Boaz are married and their new son carries on the family tradition for Naomi. In the midst of examining the text, the commentaries, and the interpretations by the women in Asia, she needed a period of listening to all the ideas swirling around in her faithful biblical scholar's mind before the text could, as she has said, "read her" and bring her thoughts to a resolution.

Sakenfeld focused on the specific cultural setting of Ruth and how the image of hope "worked" within that culture. We see, she said,

> [a vision] of community that is characterized by reciprocal movement from margin to center and from center to margin by racial/ethnic inclusiveness, and by adequate physical sustenance for all: a community of upright individuals together creating and affirming justice and mercy; a community in which weeping turns to joy and tears are wiped away; a community in which children are valued and old

people are well cared for; a community in which a daughter
is greatly valued.[29]

Her clue to a safer reading of Ruth is that "these features, rather
than their specific expression in ancient Israelite culture"[30]
make it an eschatological vision of future hope for human
community and an example of hospitality. Sakenfeld opts to
understand the book of Ruth as offering us "a memory of the
future" of God's promised redemption of all creation. Rather
than try to re-create Ruth's Judean village, readers should try to
re-create the *vision* of a community concerned for the well-
being of its inhabitants. The vision of hope in the text, high-
lighted by the "happily ever after" ending, might be viewed as
a metaphor for God's New Creation, where all are partners
with each other and God through our acts of hospitality.

Sakenfeld's Ruth experience is an example of a spirituality of
listening in biblical study that does not force a particular interpretation on the listener, but rather invites us to listen to the
conversations of our own hearts and minds. This model of
hospitality lets a space open up for us as an invitation to hear
what God might be saying to us—an offer of God's welcome.
Providing safe space for reading and understanding Scripture
demands such a spirituality of silence and attention.

Each of us needs to search out our own ways of listening,
together with the faith communities of which we are a part.
Adding listening to our hermeneutic of suspicion and commitment might help to make our interpretations safe for the text
and the text safe for us. Let me suggest that in a spirituality of
listening we might want to include at least these three components. First, we should be sure to *listen to views different from our
own*, especially those we have not heard before. Of particular
importance here is listening to the perspectives of people who
have been marginalized in society or who have suffered the violence and oppression that heightens their awareness of the dangers of the text. Postcolonial interpretation, which I discussed in
chapter 2, is one avenue into those other perspectives. Here
people living in countries of the South, in Africa, Asia, and

Latin America, read between the spaces or within the spaces, meaning they ask new questions about the social, political, and economic structures, while creating new interdependent relationships to discover the hidden messages of colonialism in the biblical messages. Musa Dube, for example, in her postcolonial interpretation of Matthew, stresses the colonial bias of Matthew as he tells the gospel story in the context of the Roman Empire.[31] In so doing they can discover the hidden and not so hidden messages of colonialism in the biblical texts. Let us reread the Great Commission in Matthew 28:19–20a: "Go therefore and make disciples of all nations, baptizing them in the name of the Father, and of the Son, and of the Holy Spirit, and teaching them to obey everything that I have commanded you." About it, Musa Dube writes:

> Because this model is expressed in absolute terms of superior, traveling teachers and dependent, student nations, the mission to the nations hardly makes room for working with and for differences among different nations. Rather, it advocates imposing sameness on a world of differences, for surely disciplining nations to "obey" all that Christ commanded makes little allowance for diverse teachings of other cultures.[32]

Second, we need to *live with the text in community*. The Bible developed over time and out of the struggles of communities of faith. Even within the canon we find contradictions and differences. The book of Ruth, for example, reinterprets things like the violence in Judges and Israelite views against intermarriage and the exclusion of foreigners. Other examples are Deuteronomy's rewriting the law of Moses as the "second law"; Matthew's writing of the teachings of Jesus in the Sermon on the Mount as a new law or guide for daily life in a Christian community; and the story of the Emmaus road, when Jesus reinterpreted the Scriptures (Luke 24:13–35). Reading the Bible is always informed by listening and discussion in community as we continue to seek out how it can speak in such different times and places.

Certainly Katharine Sakenfeld's conversations with women in various Asian countries over a period of almost three years changed the way she thought about the Bible. Even her interpretation of the book of Ruth, a text with which she was especially familiar, underwent serious changes in the way she made meaning of the text. The conversations reframed her understanding of the text.

Third, we need to *allow space for the Spirit*, the "new thing" that God might reveal through the text. This means we must not exclude any texts, even those such as Ruth and Naomi.[33] Perhaps we discover, in our reading, that the story is a powerful message *against* the daily sacrifice of human life in our societies through poverty, violence, and suffering. We don't want to look in any biblical text for "cheap hope," a hope that makes everything come out right, and this is why we must be cautious with the "happy ending" of Ruth and Naomi. Yet we know that in searching the Scriptures there is space for God's welcome—God's *just hospitality*—to break into our lives.

Like Ruth and Naomi, we are often searching for "a way out of no way," yet we can know that even in the deepest difficulty with our lives, with our world, or with the Scriptures themselves, there are spaces where the theme of God's will for hospitality and human safety breaks through.[34] Perhaps a hermeneutic of suspicion and commitment, silence and listening will assist our search for these safe spaces. And we may be surprised by the way God's love echoes through our lives and world in the face of danger and despair.

In searching for a safe space in Scripture we more clearly see certain themes and characteristics of hospitality that give us intimations of God's welcome. Ruth and Naomi are one example of that welcome as they lovingly care for each other in the midst of their grief and poverty, despite differences of ethnicity and religion. Their hospitality toward one another reframes traditional notions of hospitality—such as terminal niceness, charity without justice, and helping others with the underlying intent of making them become like us—to show us that differences are not hindrances and that God's welcome is a form of partnership with the "other."

There are a lot of reasons to be afraid to offer hospitality to the "other" or those on the margins; to fear the stranger knocking at our door, the person with a different religion, the worker taking our job in Mexico or Mozambique, or the terrorist waiting to destroy our city. Some of these fears are valid and cautionary tales. But often, even when our fears have a basis, they combine with our own insecurity and resentment and lead to hatred between different races, classes, genders, and sexual orientations. Kingman Brewster, former president of Yale University, wrote these words for the stone marker at his grave, "The presumption of innocence is not just a legal concept, in commonplace terms; it rests on that generosity of spirit which assumes the best, not the worst, in the stranger."[35]

In Romans 15:7 Paul says to Christian communities: "Welcome one another, therefore, just as Christ has welcomed you, for the glory of God." In the East Harlem Protestant Parish where I worked, we tried to remind ourselves of Paul's advice by asking church members to put a particular sticker on their doors: The sticker had a cross, with crossed hands, and both above and below the cross were these words:

Welcome in the name of Christ. Bienvenido en el nombre de Cristo.

Even though every door had at least two locks, and probably a police lock as well, it was important that residents resist the alienation of city life. For the welcome of Christ extends far beyond our sanctuaries to the strangers who may never come to a church service, yet are looking for someone who can understand their language and their problems. Those of us who respond to our own insecurity by living in fear of those who are different, cut ourselves off from our neighbors and their real or imagined differences.

Questions for Thought

1. In what ways have you or your community of faith sought to partner with persons less advantaged than you and/or those in your church?
2. Why is it important to examine how we read Scripture? What are the dangers when we don't? Has the way in which you read Scripture changed over time? Has that change been conscious? Unconscious? What motivated it?
3. How does Scripture help us to define our practice of hospitality?
4. What "signs" similar to *Bienvenido en el nombre de Cristo* do you post to resist inhospitality in our society? What "signs" does your church post?

5
Just Hospitality

Just hospitality is the practice of God's welcome by reaching out across difference to participate in God's actions bringing justice and healing in our world of crisis and fear of the ones we call "other." To live out God's welcome as just hospitality is a calling and a challenge. As strangers ourselves, and strangers to so many other people, we have the possibility of partnering with others as a sign of God's concern for us all, and for all creation. Hospitality is not *the only* answer to difference, but it is a challenge to us, pointing us to a future that God intends, where riotous difference is welcomed. After the September 11, 2001, attacks, Chief Rabbi Sir Jonathan Sacks of the United Hebrew Congregations of the Commonwealth shared his Jewish New Year message:

> I used to think that the greatest command in the Bible was "You shall love your neighbour as yourself." I was wrong. Only in one place does the Bible ask us to love our neighbour. In more than thirty places it commands us to love the stranger. Don't oppress the stranger because you know what it feels like to be a stranger—you were once strangers in the

land of Egypt. It isn't hard to love our neighbours because by and large our neighbours are people like us. What's tough is to love the stranger, the person who isn't like us, who has a different skin colour, or a different faith, or a different background. That's the real challenge. It was in ancient times. It still is today.[1]

The basis of this practice of hospitality is that we were once strangers, exiles, nobodies and are now welcomed by God so that we might welcome others. At the same time, hospitality is a gift in which we discover the presence of God in our mutual interaction with the stranger, as did Abraham and Sarah at the oaks of Mamre (Gen. 18:1–15). The Greek New Testament abounds in exhortations to hospitality as well, and Matthew 25:31–46 tells us that Christ promises to be present to us through our actions of solidarity with the stranger. As we know, the relationship between a stranger and the person or people offering hospitality is not one of equal power. *Just hospitality* requires us to recognize the "otherness" in the relationship of hospitality and to respond in a manner reflective of God's welcoming example.

UNEQUALLY YOKED

Inclusion is certainly a linchpin of any definition of hospitality. Perhaps we each know best our own tradition, and so I look now at what a theologian from my own denomination, the Presbyterian Church (U.S.A.), has said about the issue of inclusion.

Any believable theology of "welcome" must somehow seek to achieve real welcome, a real reaching out to the Other in word and deed—especially the "Other" whom we find most difficult to embrace, the one over there on the other side of the aisle.[2]

With this generous description of hospitality Professor William Stacy Johnson of Princeton Theological Seminary concludes his appeal that all factions in the Presbyterian Church (U.S.A.) be "equally yoked" in their willingness to be open to one another. He penned this statement in the "Table Talk" section of *Presbyterian Outlook*, a journal of the denomination. His choice of the phrase "equally yoked" is interesting, for he turns inside out the translation of a phrase in 2 Corinthians 6:14, found in the King James and American Standard versions of the Bible. There Paul writes "Be not unequally yoked with unbelievers: for what fellowship have righteousness and iniquity? Or what communion hath light with darkness?" Certainly hospitality was not on Paul's mind when he uttered this warning. In Johnson's favor, he changes the adjective from unequal to equal, but are the parties in fact equal, or are they still unequal? Those denied ordination because of their sexual preference are asked to join with those opposing their ordination in order to follow Johnson's idea that they should be equally yoked.

He wrote these remarks in response to a document entitled Affirmation 2001, and they are worded with care and rooted in the denomination's historic 1923 Auburn Affirmation, which was written in opposition to fundamentalism in the Presbyterian Church. The Auburn Affirmation was a response to the requirements imposed by the Presbyterian General Assemblies of 1910, 1916, and 1923 requiring candidates for ordination to be asked five questions dealing with articles considered fundamental to the faith. These concerned such issues as the virgin birth, biblical inerrancy, and Christ's physical second coming. At the turn of the twenty-first century and in a similar manner, a group gathered several times in Baltimore, New York, and San Francisco, to answer a call from the Reverend David Bos to create a new Auburn Affirmation. As one of the many drafters of this document, eventually titled Affirmation 2001, and an enthusiastic signer, I will use it to clarify the meaning of hospitality when persons in a dialogue are "unequally yoked."

Professor Johnson writes about hospitality and equal regard from a position of the "superior middle." As a male, heterosexual professor at Princeton he is able to stand back, reflect on the issues, and point out that both sides are wrong and need to get along together. For those like me, whose standing in the church is in question because of the church's legislation and practice, it is difficult to see how we are equally yoked. Although, for instance, I was ordained in 1958 and have served the church since 1951 as a pastor and educator, I am no longer eligible to be a pastor in any Presbyterian church because I am a lesbian. My fifty-plus years of service are invalidated by the present constitution.

There is no way that the many persons who have served or would like to serve the church but are presently excluded because of issues of sexuality can consider themselves equally yoked with other groups in the church. Johnson also says that we need to come to theological consensus on "gay ordination" before moving to polity considerations. When the question of ordination of gay and lesbian persons came to the General Assembly in 1978, it was decided to move away from polity and instead study the issue. We were still studying it in 1991, when the church refused the Human Sexuality report. Backlash has been around a long time, and many of us are very tired of waiting for the church to open its heart to us. In a diverse church there never will be just one theological interpretation of issues of Christian faith and life, but practicing hospitality would lead us to recognize and respect differing interpretations and stop legislating people's faith.

There is a *crisis in the church*, and that crisis has to do with "one faction's inability to affirm Christ's presence in the lives and ministries of all faithful Presbyterians."[3] Those who signed Affirmation 2001 were not trying to exclude any group. Rather, they said that all persons who declare their faith in the Lord Jesus Christ should be welcome as members and eligible to be officers in this church. The historic nature of the church itself is in crisis when new criteria are established for membership in the church beyond that of faith in Jesus Christ.

This brings us to the question of how one *does* practice hospitality among persons who are "unequally yoked." I couldn't agree more with Dr. Johnson when he describes hospitality as a biblical theme that is "a statement of who God is and of who we are called to be as the people of God."[4] God's hospitality toward all of us and all creation in Jesus Christ is the cornerstone of the gospel message of good news to all who have been "the despised, the rejected, the neighbor in need."[5] What is missing from the idea of "equally yoked," however, is the acknowledgment that the practice of hospitality does not begin with the preservation of unity at the expense of those already excluded. Some who have served the church as pastors their whole lives long cannot, for example, leave their pension to their partner, should they die. Similarly, health benefits are denied to partners in relationships that are not heterosexual. Here the Presbyterian Church is behind other parts of U.S. society, where oftentimes partners are included in pensions and health-care benefits.

Instead, hospitality begins when we seek to welcome one another in Christ by taking very seriously the social situations of our lives and those of other persons. There are many factors that lead people to disagree. It is not just doctrine, or just Scripture, or just the community of faith. It is our differing class, race, gender, ability, age, and sexual identity and orientation. It is also the way each of us individually has been taught to understand the gospel message. It is political ideologies that feed on people's fears and insecurities, as well as their need to be "right." To welcome another person or group is to look beneath the surface of what they say and do, to understand "where they are coming from," and to address the social context out of which the conversation comes. If we think someone is being used by those who would manipulate that person, we need to take the person and the possibility seriously, not just dismiss it or dismiss them. If we hear a person crying out in fear, hospitality includes addressing the issues of fear, not just offering comfort.

When we extend a welcome to others on the basis of hearing and learning and trusting in the possibility that Christ is present in the other persons, we will hear a gospel that is situation variable, just as it was in Jesus' day. For instance, for the deaf, the news that the blind could see was nice, but not as nice as it was for the person who was blind. This good news from

Christ will call some to repent, some to stand up and walk, some to share a gift, or pray without ceasing. For the church to practice this form of hospitality in Christ, it must be open to the full participation of all persons. In this church we will no longer find "them and us," but all those whom Christ has called in many and various ways to be together in a very diverse community of faith.

JUSTICE IN "JUST" HOSPITALITY

Our struggles to overcome the fear of difference and to "break all the bars that still keep us apart" challenge our local, national, and global institutions to practice hospitality with justice. Christian hospitality is more than a cheery smile from the sunshine lady. It includes providing food, clothing, and shelter to the homeless and welcoming strangers in our sanctuaries. But it also includes actions of genuine solidarity with those who are different from us. It goes beyond caring for the other to enabling them to care for themselves and others.

The sort of hospitality that makes this possible would be one that sees the struggle for justice as part and parcel of welcoming the stranger. According to Robert McAfee Brown, if you read your Bible you will discover that *justice* appears to be God's middle name![6] God's justice, or putting things right, includes the absence of oppression, not just the presence of distributive rights.[7] Difference is the gift that challenges us to practice such hospitality by resisting oppression and working for full human life and dignity for those with whom we stand in solidarity.

Justice, then, requires a practice of solidarity to end oppressions beyond working for individual access and insurance of rights. In defining the practice of justice, I am reminded of the reciprocal description of justice and love that my colleague Margaret Farley articulates. In her most recent book, *Just Love: A Framework for Christian Sexual Ethics*,[8] she observes that justice and love are not two separate actions. Rather, love *includes* justice in the care for other persons, and justice *includes* love in our relationships. When this is not the case, a person receives care that lacks concern for their total well-being and the removal of the causes of their predicament. On the flip side, actions for justice with no concern for whom they harm or heal result in social structures that ignore the fabric of human relationships. In other words, justice and love flow into each other and are necessary components of each other. God's welcome is then an act of both love and justice through the offer of unbounded hospitality.

Amos's Message

To illustrate the connection between justice and hospitality further, picture the Sunday worship in your church. Are the women singing in the choir and caring for those who need prayer? Are the men preaching and counting the offering? Who decides about the worship service or liturgy and the language used for God and men and women? Who is not there and not welcome in the service? How many people of different classes, races, or community groups attend worship? These are questions many of us ask of our worship services as we seek to reflect God's way of justice and hospitality. And we begin to discover that our worship usually reflects our community's culturally assigned roles of gender, race, and class. These are also the sort of questions that the prophet Amos was asking long ago when he found that the worship at Bethel in northern Israel reflected the injustices in the Israelite community, rather than God's way of justice and hospitality.

Amos was the earliest of a series of prophets, known to us through their writings in the Hebrew Scriptures, who first arose in the eighth century BCE to confront the unfaithfulness and injustices of the people of Israel and Judah. They called the people to be faithful to the God who had delivered them from exile in Egypt and had formed a covenant of righteousness that recognized God's authority over the actions of kings as well as peasants.

Amos was a shepherd, or herdsman, and fig cutter who cared for his flocks in Tekoa, a smaller fortress town in Judah, south of Jerusalem. He did not belong to the priests or the group of prophets who served sanctuaries in Judah and Israel (Amos 7:14–15), and we don't know much about him. In fact, all we know is that he received a call from God to prophesy and crossed over the border into Israel. At the royal sanctuary at Bethel he proclaimed God's word of judgment against a people whose worship reflected a culture of affluence and ease for the rich and poverty and oppression for the poor. And like other prophets and like Jesus himself, he was rejected along with his message (Luke 4:16–30). Amaziah, the temple priest, considered Amos's message heresy and sedition against the king and attempted to expel him and report him to the royal authorities (Amos 7:10–17).

Amos's message of impending destruction is the message many remember from Scripture—because it came true. But his more abiding message is God's call for healing and justice in our communities and in the world around us. Thus in Amos 5:21–24 Amos proclaims God's message. He condemns religious festivals and "solemn assemblies" because they conceal a complacent community, full of economic and legal injustices, that no longer looks to God as its guide to righteousness and justice. He is demanding that in their life and in their worship people be life-giving to all: "But let justice roll down like waters, and righteousness like an everflowing stream" (Amos 5:24).

Amos's call for justice goes out to people in his community, but only certain people were in his consciousness—the elite, the powerful—the oppressed were not part of the problem or the solution. For his justice call to be effective, he must also be aware of the social context within which he lives; justice is more than distributive rights or correcting behavior, it is concerned with ending oppression.

So what was going on in Israel and Judah? The Hebrew people had become divided into two nations, the stronger northern kingdom of Israel and the weaker southern kingdom of Judah. Each kingdom had its own king, and there was a great deal of political strife between the two nations, which had formerly been unified under the rule of King David and King Solomon. Constant harassment and strife defined their international relationships with neighboring nations as well as with the larger nations that dominated Israel and Judah—Assyria in the North and Egypt in the South. Soon after the prophecy of Amos in about 760 BCE, this strife led to the fall of the northern kingdom in 721 and the southern kingdom in 586, along with the exile of many of the Hebrew people.

Within the two nations the hierarchical structures of kingship and the developing economic structures of trade stratified the society. The kings, the royal court, and the elite copied the social structures of the surrounding and more powerful nations, where those at the top lived in luxury and those at the bottom in abject poverty and despair. The wealthy ignored the signs of external danger and believed that God's covenant with Israel would protect their nations, no matter what other nations did or whether the people abandoned the old traditions of justice and care for all the people. Their religion had become a comfortable ritual divorced from God's demands for justice.

Economic injustice had led to exploitation and slavery, and Amos speaks God's word against Israel's transgressions.

> Thus says the LORD:
> For three transgressions of Israel,
>   and for four, I will not revoke the punishment;
> because they sell the righteous for silver,
>   and the needy for a pair of sandals.
>   (Amos 2:6)

Justice in the courts was perverted in favor of the rich. About the people who gathered at the gate for court cases, Amos says,

> . . . And how great are your sins—
> you who afflict the righteous, who take a bribe,
>   and push aside the needy in the gate.
>   (Amos 5:12)

Yet despite his words of condemnation, even in Amos's prophesying, he speaks *out of* and *to* a patriarchal community.

Take, for example, his use of evil women, as a scapegoat for the
sins of the people. He mentions the sins of elite women whom
he calls, "cows of Bashan," but ignores the particular hardships of
poor women in times of war, or circumstances of great poverty
and injustice toward the poor. His only other mention of women
is as wives and daughters of the men he addresses (7:17). Amos
emphasizes justice, to be sure, but he gives no thought to gender
justice in his oracles. Similar blinders are often worn today,
when, for example, women are scapegoated for the evils of the
community—for example, women with HIV/AIDS in Africa,
the mothers of children who grow up as delinquents in the
United States, and wives in Korea who fail the family because no
male heir is born. The problems of Amos's time read like our
daily newspaper, portraying the daily struggles of people and
nations around the world. The full participation of women is
needed in the struggle to find paths to healing and justice.

Although righteousness and justice are two different words
in both Hebrew and English, they are used by Amos and other
Hebrew writers in ways that are synonymous. Righteousness
(*sedaqah*) means the standard for what is right according to the
laws and traditions of Moses and the people of Israel. Justice
(*mishpat*) is the realization of those standards in our lives as we
love God and our neighbor. Amos calls upon both the laws and
traditions—righteousness and the act of realizing those standards—and justice in the parallel poetry of 5:24, as well as 6:12:

> But you have turned justice into poison
> and the fruit of righteousness into wormwood.
> (Amos 6:12)

In other words, God has made a covenant with Israel, and
that covenant faithfulness, or loyalty, is to be expressed by
God's people through righteousness and includes material as
well as social well-being. Because God is just in keeping a right
relationship with the people of Israel and the whole creation,
the people are to be just in their relationships to other persons,
animals, and the natural environment. The righteousness of

God means that *God puts things right* as the creator and sustainer of the world.

The justice of God is not only about giving each person their due; it is about the restoration of right relationships and about God's judgment on those who are unjust. For instance, Amos declares that the day of God's vindication will be a day of judgment, because people have broken the covenant (5:18–24). Religious leaders and religious communities are included in this call to heal relationships and live according to the design of God, in which women and men were created to image God as equal partners in the care of the earth (Gen. 1:27).

Justice as Hospitality in Worship

With Amos's biblical example in mind, let's return to my original questions about our worship experiences. We all have a long way to go to have our worship and our lives express God's just hospitality. But as we ask ourselves about the things most needing justice and healing in our own churches, we can still know deeply that there is *no separation* between things spiritual and material, religious and political, sacred and secular in our lives. God is in all of it, calling us to make connections and work on mending our lives, churches, and world. Amos's story provides at least three clues to working toward a more just community.

First, *worship cannot be separated from the rest of our lives.* We must pay attention to the social context, as Amos did in his calls for justice. Worship gives praise to God insofar as it mirrors the efforts of the congregation to give praise in their lives as well. Worship can, for example, become death-dealing rather than life-giving when it teaches women that they are inferior to men and makes them a scapegoat for unrighteousness. This is happening over and over, when, for instance, some churches in Africa ignore the issues of human sexuality, the status of women, and poverty, and preach that HIV/AIDS is God's punishment on sinners. Their message ignores the plight of the many children, caregivers, faithfully married women, and powerless, sexually exploited women who are infected. The question that is asked by women and justice-seeking men in these and other churches around the world is whether the theology of their communities is *life-giving*, calling for healing and justice rather than condemnation.

Second, *healing cannot be separated from justice*. When we call for healing and reconciliation between peoples, religions, nations, women and men, we are not calling persons to conform to the pattern of the most dominant group doing the calling. There is no way to heal from violence, terror, or brokenness if the injustice that caused the problem is not also addressed. This is why Amos so clearly names the economic injustices and the faults of courts in his day. If a nation such as the United States wants to eliminate terrorism, it needs to do more than use military force and destruction, for terrorism at its base is a response to political, economic, and religious injustice and will disappear only when communities demonstrate respect for human rights and right relationship among peoples.

Last, *gender justice cannot be separated from other forms of justice*. If we want to change the role of women in their homes and churches, we must prioritize gender justice: just relations between women and men in their communities. In the patriarchal culture that existed in Amos's time, the call for justice focused mostly on the needs and perspectives of the dominant men in the community and was expressed through forecasts of war and destruction. But then and now, and in all our communities, there is no possibility of just relations to one another, to creation, or to God if justice is denied to half of the human race. This applies to worship and conduct alike.

Amos was called to speak God's word of healing and justice. This is the same calling that we continue to receive as women and men (Acts 2:14–21). It is God's call to each of us to seek out ways to live in just relationships among ourselves and with God, to live out Amos's vision of justice rolling down like waters "and righteousness like an everflowing stream" (Amos 5:24). There is still hope for all of us, hope that one day we will be a voice for justice among the oppressed of every nation. We reflect this hope in our worship. It seems to be an impossible possibility (see chapter 3), which may come to pass, for God is at work in the world to help us learn what it means to welcome the stranger as God has welcomed us.

Our world is full of structures of domination that cannot be altered without attention to social, political, economic, and religious factors. For instance, the AIDS pandemic in Africa incorporates many factors, such as colonial and neocolonial exploitation, gender inequality, ecological destruction, poverty, harmful cultural practices, political instability, and the lack of health care, to name only some.[9] Each of these individual dilemmas must be attended to in the practice of hospitality and healing, even though that practice begins with one family, one medicine, one act of just hospitality at a time.

HOSPITALITY IN JUST HOSPITALITY

In the midst of fear and danger we seek safety in God and the assurance that the "everlasting arms of God" do not abandon us. At the same time, we look to our neighbor and remember that the One who convicts us of God's Welcome bids us, in the words of Romans 15:7, to "welcome one another as Christ has welcomed us." Welcome has been personified as ways of speaking about God's presence in our world, as Jesus Christ who embodies that welcome among us. Christ is God's Welcome because in the life, death, and resurrection of Jesus Christ we are invited to trust God's love for us. Given the events of the last decade, with the terrorist attacks in the United States and the bombing terror in Afghanistan, Christ as God's Welcome is a metaphor that connects with our lives.

Welcome as a Metaphor for Action

Christ as God's Welcome is a metaphor for God's action in reaching out to us and for our response. In Luke, Jesus is pictured moving from house to house, and table to table. Even as the risen Christ, Jesus returns to break bread at Emmaus and to eat fish in a Jerusalem room (Luke 24). Our own story of Christian community is also constructed around ways of expressing God's hospitality, not only with one another, but with all of God's creatures and creation. In 1997 a group of Presbyterians felt called to form a group called the Covenant Network to encourage support for a change to the church constitution to allow the ordination of lesbian, gay, bisexual, and transgendered ministers of the Word and Sacrament, elders, and deacons. They invited churches and individuals to sign "A Call to Covenant Community," which affirms that

> the church we seek to strengthen is built upon the hospitality of Jesus, who said, "Whoever comes to me I will not cast out." The good news of the gospel is that all—those who are near and those who were far off—are invited; all are members of the household and citizens of the realm of God.[10]

God's hospitality in a world of difference and danger is the source of our life, and it is not an optional action for us or our churches.[11]

The table we gather around is a symbol of God's hospitality in welcoming strangers, persons who are on the margins of our churches and cultures.[12] Not only at Communion, but at Ground Zero serving coffee and sandwiches; in soup kitchens, hospitals, and prisons; as well as at potluck dinners, family reunions, and conferences, we gather to share bread, and recognize Christ's presence in our midst. Jesus welcomes all.

Transforming God's Welcome

The metaphor of Christ as God's Welcome is particularly important to those of us who feel that we are in danger or crisis. The power of the metaphor is dependent on what is happening in our lives and world, and in this culture. As I have said, the gospel is situation variable. Knowing this gives us

an important clue to our understanding of H. Richard Niebuhr's phrase "Christ transforming culture." *Transformation is
a two-way street.* As Niebuhr recognized, culture is always
changing, and we are constantly needing to give an account of
our faith in Jesus Christ in new circumstances. We draw our
theologies out of biblical and church tradition, and we develop
careful arguments for what we believe, but ultimately they
have to be *seriously imaginable* to people in a particular time
and culture.[13]

Transformation is a two-way street in that *both our culture
and our Christology are being transformed.* Reimagining Christ,
or making Christ the metaphor of God's Welcome, requires
speaking to the hearts and minds of the growing diversity in
culture and religion, both in this country and abroad, and thus
transforming culture as we put our metaphor into action. The
metaphor also has the potential of transforming our understanding of Christ's presence in our lives. That is why typolo-
gies never precisely fit our reality but only provide guidelines
for looking at Christ and culture in an ever-changing land-
scape. In other words, the story of Jesus' life, death, and resurrection does not change, but, by the power of the Holy Spirit,
our Christologies transform along with culture and community, making God's Welcome clear to us in our current context.

If we want the church to matter in the twenty-first century,
we must become a community that practices God's Welcome
and hospitality in a world of difference and danger. Perhaps
in this matter we can give H. Richard Niebuhr the last word.
When discussing the paradox of sin and grace in culture, he
tells us that love is an *impossible possibility.*[14] If so, then in
God's grace, it is an impossible possibility that *the church will
matter* in the years to come! As I have said, although the
church is one in Christ, it lives each day torn by difference. It
lives each day with the impossible possibility that one day God
will fulfill the unity of the church and mend the creation that
has been so torn apart. Our actions of just hospitality begin
that mending.

RECOGNIZING JUST HOSPITALITY

To live out God's Welcome in our worship, our church, our lives is no easy task. That is why I continue to reiterate the concept of impossible possibility; we are called beyond what we believe are our limitations to live into a greater possibility. You probably know from your own reflection and experience that there are limitations on our practice of hospitality, many of which we have already discussed. First, there is the limitation of *the term "hospitality"* itself. For instance, as Christine Pohl says, it is no longer perceived as an essential aspect of Christian faith and practice, but often is connected to personal entertainment, the hospitality industry, and the use of women's bodies for sexual favors or financial gain.[15] Second, difference is used as a way of excluding and dominating persons because of their race, class, gender, sexual orientation, nationality, and more. For instance, we see class difference in a *dualistic frame of reference* when hospitality toward the poor is used to justify the superiority of those giving the aid. Last, hospitality is limited by the ways we practice it, the boundaries we place around it, and the temptations we find to abuse it. Let us turn now to look at three areas in which we learn to limit hospitality: personal relationships, social structures, and theological traditions.

Limits

Personal limits to hospitality include such things as burnout, limited resources, including space and money, finitude of those offering hospitality and the strings that are attached to the hospitality, and its misuse to reinforce the power of the givers over the receivers. I have referred to this as "deformation of hospitality."[16] *Social structural limits* include the need to have a place to offer hospitality and to maintain it and the need of a community to have an identity in order to offer hospitality. Last, a need exists for boundaries that keep both the guest and workers safe. The *limits of the theological tradition* include doctrines that exclude nonmembers or declare that only certain people are saved.

We need to remember that just hospitality is a *relation-ship* that is rooted in our God-given human nature; it is not a commodity to be rationed. As British theologian Mary Grey points out, the fundamental activity of God is relational, as seen in the community of the Trinity, and in our creation as relational beings, in the *image of God*.[17] It is *our need* to limit that makes us ask the question first off: "What about limits?" "What must I do to be saved?" (Matt. 16:19–22). When we think in a dualistic and hierarchical way about who is in or out, we also are more concerned about boundaries than about the center and meaning of our common life. There are limits, but they are ours. We need to be realistic, so we can be part of these relationships of care, but we also do not need to limit God's welcome.

A better way to think theologically is to ask how our practice of hospitality can be nourished and strengthened in relationships that point to God's concern to mend the creation and that are a sign of God's care, rather than a focus on human limitations. We know that what we do is inadequate, but we include God in the relationship, confident that the mending can be brought about by God, despite our limited efforts of hospitality. Hospitality is a gift of God to us, one that we need to practice, so that we are more open to its blessing. Like the gifts of faith, hope, and love, hospitality has to be used. It is a relationship to be shared, not buried in a field, or in our studies, or in our jobs. Hospitality builds relationships across difference and in this way is a catalyst for community that is built out of difference. In the words of the hymn by Doreen Potter and Fred Kaan:

> Help us accept each other as Christ accepted us:
> Teach us as sister, brother, each person to embrace.
> Be present, Lord, among us and bring us to believe
> We are ourselves accepted and meant to love and live.[18]

Even as we share together our own limitations, boundaries, and temptations, we can give thanks for God's just hospitality.

Essential Characteristics

The practice of just hospitality in a world of difference as I have laid it out does not make it easy to find unity across the many barriers that divide us from one another, but it provides the possibility of moving closer to unity. It pushes us to welcome many perspectives, and might even come out of much struggle and pain. Practicing just hospitality by recognizing and accepting difference would have a different look to it from practicing hospitality as we do it in the church today. I believe there are four underlying understandings essential to the practice of just hospitality in a world of difference: (1) clarity of mission, (2) reexamination of the Bible and traditions, (3) an alliance of partnership and power, and (4) the goal of justice. If we incorporate these into our practice in the church and in our lives, the face of hospitality will change, and there will be a shift in the ways we work together in our churches, our homes, our communities, and our world. Let's briefly *imagine* what such a shift might look like as we practice hospitality in a world of difference. Then I will leave it to you to ask how hospitality happens in your own churches, institutions, and communities.

1. **Clarity of mission.** Hospitality is best practiced when we are clear about both our own mission as a church or institution and the importance of living out God's hospitality to us in the ways we break down barriers between ourselves and other people. When we do this, we have a distinct understanding of where we are headed, why our mission is important, and how it is in line with the biblical call for justice and hospitality. For instance, the work of Presbyterian Promise in the Presbytery of Southern New England is committed to getting the word out that not all Presbyterians reject "queer" persons and that many Presbyterians treat such persons as their neighbors, friends, and fellow church members. We are recognized as an advocacy group of the presbytery, not because everyone agrees with our stance of welcome and inclusion, but because the majority do agree that this perspective is an important part of the outreach or mission